PENGUIN ANANDA
A TREASURY OF INDIAN WISDOM

Dr Karan Singh was born heir apparent to the state of Jammu and Kashmir and served successively as regent, Sardar-i-Riyasat and governor of the state. A Padma Vibhushan, Dr Singh has held the portfolios for tourism and civil aviation, health and family planning, and education and culture in the Indian government, and served as ambassador to the United States. He has been chairman of the Committee on Ethics of the Rajya Sabha. As chancellor, he has been affiliated to the Jammu and Kashmir University, the Jawaharlal Nehru University and the Banaras Hindu University. He has chaired the Indian Board of Wildlife and the India International Centre.

Presently, he is chairman of the governing board of the Auroville Foundation and was India's representative on the UNESCO executive board for many years. Associated with several cultural and academic institutions, he composes and recites devotional songs in Dogri and is a connoisseur of Indian classical music.

His published works include his *Autobiography*, *Essays on Hinduism*, *An Examined Life*, as well as his extensive correspondence with Pandit Jawaharlal Nehru in *Jammu and Kashmir 1949–64* and Mrs Indira Gandhi in *Kashmir and Beyond 1966–84*.

A
Treasury *of*
Indian
Wisdom

KARAN SINGH

PENGUIN
ANANDA

An imprint of Penguin Random House

PENGUIN ANANDA

USA | Canada | UK | Ireland | Australia
New Zealand | India | South Africa | China

Penguin Ananda is part of the Penguin Random House group of companies
whose addresses can be found at global.penguinrandomhouse.com

Published by Penguin Random House India Pvt. Ltd
4th Floor, Capital Tower 1, MG Road,
Gurugram 122 002, Haryana, India

First published in Penguin Ananda by Penguin Books India 2010
Paperback edition published 2015
This edition published 2020

ISBN 9780143426158

Typeset in Dante MT Std by InoSoft Systems, Noida

Printed at Repro India Limited

www.penguin.co.in

To Asha
Swasti wah paraya tamasah parastit
(May your journey towards the light be auspicious)

and

To all the great minds whose thoughts appear in this book,
with deep respect and gratitude

CONTENTS

Introduction   ix

THE VEDANTA

NASADIYA SUKTA   3
PRAYER FOR LONG LIFE   5
HYMN TO THE EARTH   6
ISA UPANISHAD   18
CHANDOGYA UPANISHAD   21
SHVETASHVATARA UPANISHAD   32
MUNDAKA UPANISHAD   40

THE GREAT REVOLTS

JAIN TEXTS   51
BUDDHIST TEXTS   57

THE ACHARYAS

BHAGVAD GITA   71
KALIDASA   77
SHANKARACHARYA   80
SAIVITE SAINTS   84

BASAVANNA   91
TULSIDAS   109

To the Formless One

AMIR KHUSRAU   113
KABIR   115
SHAIKH NIZAM UD-DIN AULIYA   118
DARA SHIKOH   122
GURU NANAK   127
GURU GOBIND SINGH   133

The Moderns

MIRZA GHALIB   143
RAMMOHUN ROY   147
SWAMI VIVEKANANDA   152
SRI AUROBINDO   154
RABINDRANATH TAGORE   162
MOHANDAS KARAMCHAND GANDHI   166
MUHAMMAD IQBAL   172
MAULANA ABUL KALAM AZAD   180
JAWAHARLAL NEHRU   191
J. KRISHNAMURTI   199
OSHO   202

Sources   213
Copyright Acknowledgements   214

INTRODUCTION

INTRODUCTION

The Indic civilization is by far the longest surviving civilization on this planet. There have been earlier ones, such as the Pharaonic in Egypt, but they have disappeared leaving behind only magnificent monuments but no human contacts. In India, however, for at least five millenia, from the earliest Vedas, there has been an unbroken tradition of spiritual, religious and literary output which is astonishing in its vibrancy and sheer profusion. The Mahabharata itself is longer than both the Iliad and the Odyssey combined, and that represents but a small fraction of our scriptural heritage.

Apart from its antiquity and magnitude, a special feature of Indian culture has been its extreme diversity and plurality, covering not only 5000 continuing years of Hinduism but also other great religions including Jainism, Buddhism, Islam and Sikhism. In each one of these, India has produced scholars and saints who have enriched world literature by their outpourings both in poetry and in prose. Additionally, there have been 'secular' writings which are also absorbing and replete with wisdom.

Each one of the segments of our heritage would run into multiple volumes, but what was needed was a selection of outstanding essays and poems reflecting the beauty and vibrant diversity of Indian wisdom based upon the ancient Rig Vedic dictum—*Ekam sadvipraha bahudha vadanti*—the Truth is one, the Wise call it by many names. This volume attempts to give a kaleidoscopic view of the Indian civilizational tradition with selections from the Vedas and the Upanishads, Jainism and Buddhism, Islam and Sikhism, as well as from the Indian renaissance in the eighteenth century down to the twentieth century.

We live in an era of great turmoil and transition, when old certitudes are disappearing and there is a quest for new paradigms, particularly among younger people. At a time like this it is useful to remind ourselves of the tremendously rich, vibrant, diverse and pluralistic heritage that has come down to us through the long and tortuous corridors of time. In the quest for the new, let us not fail to take advantage of the magnificent panorama of Indian thought that represents our multifaceted civilization. It is my hope that this volume will help to bring some of these gems to the consciousness of present and future generations so that they can inspire our hearts and illuminate our minds to meet whatever challenges may lie ahead, whether individual or collective.

For obvious reasons, the bulk of this anthology consists of translations from the original texts into English, and it is only in the last section that we come across works originally written in this language. Translations can seldom do justice to the original, but it has been my attempt to try and choose the most readable and eloquent translations available, and, whenever I have thought necessary, to take the liberty of doing some myself. Any attempt to present a volume of this nature is full of challenges, because the selections inevitably have to be made by a single person with all his limitations, and will surely be open to criticism. However, I have tried to the best of my ability to produce an anthology that would be of interest to educated laypersons, not only in India but around the world where, with our recent economic growth, interest in Indian civilization is growing apace.

We begin our exploration into the ocean of Indian wisdom, of course, with the Vedas. They represent the oldest extant spiritual literature in the world and consist of thousands of beautiful hymns in Sanskrit addressed to various deities but also looking deeper into the mystery of creation itself. The 'Nasadiya Sukta' is a most extraordinary statement questioning whether or not the creator Himself knows the origins of the universe. The sixty-three verses of the 'Bhumi Suktam', the 'Hymn to the Earth' in the Atharva Veda, are startling in their contemporary relevance to the ecological crisis that humanity is facing. The Vedas lead logically on to the Vedanta which is a generic term for the most profound and inspiring spiritual literature anywhere in the world, the Upanishads. These represent a series of dialogues between great teachers and worthy students, through which higher knowledge emerges. The Upanishads are texts of such beauty that it is very difficult to do them justice in a translation. Nonetheless we have sought to include a fairly broad spectrum of texts including complete shorter Upanishads and extracts from the longer ones. These present great truths in the form of narratives and actual dialogues that give them a peculiar immediacy. From the Bhagvad Gita we have chosen a less well-known chapter, but one which I have always found fascinating—Chapter 10 entitled 'Vibhuti Yoga'. It beautifully describes the fact that the divine presence manifests itself in multiple ways, not only in human beings but also in birds and animals, trees and seasons, rivers and mountains.

It is significant to note that the Indic religions—Hindusim, Jainism and Buddhism—are all dialogic religions, which implies a creative interchange of views and questions between teacher and pupil. Another special feature of the Indic religions, particularly Hinduism, is that they are not based on the teachings of any one person or one text written in any one point in time. This gives them a great deal of flexibility and adaptability to changing situations.

The second section in our anthology has been entitled 'The Great Revolts', referring to Jainism and Buddhism which were, in a way, responses to the teachings of the Vedanta. Whereas the Vedanta by definition accepts the primacy and infallibility of the Vedas, and are hence called Atmavad, Jainism and Buddhism both reject the Vedas, the former postulating millions of separate entities, Anekantavad, and the latter rejecting any immortal inner being, Anatmavad. We have chosen significant pieces from the Jain tradition, including from a great classic in Tamil—the Four Hundred Quatrains. In Buddhism we have presented the Four Noble Truths which represent the foundation of all the various schools of Buddhism, and have also included the Edicts of the great Buddhist Emperor Ashoka.

The third section entitled 'The Acharyas' refers to post-Vedic Hinduism as expounded by great thinkers such as Shankaracharya, Basavanna and the Nayanmars, the Shaiva saints who spearheaded the devotional path to salvation through worship of Lord Shiva at around the time the greatest Shiva temples were being constructed in Thanjavur, Chidambaram and elsewhere in Tamil Nadu. This was also the period when the truths and verities of the Vedanta were expressed by saints around the country in the local language, and it was this movement from Devavani (Sanskrit) to Lokvani (people's language) that triggered the great devotional upsurge that swept India cutting across barriers of class, creed and even religion itself.

We have entitled the fourth chapter 'The Formless God' and have included both Islam and Sikhism in this category. The great poems of Amir Khusrau, the wisdom of Kabir and the glowing text of the Japji Sahib are to be found here. The whole Sufi tradition flourished in India, and it has produced some of the most significant Sufi poets and saints. Among the former, Khwaja Amir Khusrau, a multifaceted genius, holds a place of pride, while for the latter, the leadership goes to Khwaja Moinuddin Chisti whose famous dargah in Ajmer is probably the most important Muslim pilgrimage after Mecca and Medina. It is significant that to this day millions of devotees, cutting across religious barriers, flock to Sufi shrines around the country. In Kashmir, particularly, the Shaiva tradition highlighted by Acharya Abhinavagupta and coming down to the great woman saint Lalleshwari, and the Sufi tradition epitomized by Sheikh Nooruddin Noorani whose dargah is in Chrar-i-Sharief combined to form the Rishi cult that has dominated the valley for centuries. From Sikhism we have taken the Japji Sahib and poems by Guru Gobind Singh.

The fifth chapter is entitled 'The Moderns' and begins with the immortal poetry of Mirza Ghalib, and goes on to include Raja Rammohun Roy, Swami Vivekananda, Sri Aurobindo, Maulana Abul Kalam Azad, Gandhiji and Jawaharlal Nehru. J. Krishnamurti, whose luminous writings inspired generations around the world, and the controversial Osho, who produced some beautiful and inspiring works, conclude this section.

It is, of course, virtually impossible to cover in a single volume any substantial fraction of our tremendously rich spiritual literary heritage going back to the very dawn of our civilization. What we have tried to do here is to present a representative selection which would illustrate the multifaceted, pluralistic and inclusive nature of our heritage. The need for such a book is now urgently felt because whole generations have grown up without even a faint acquaintance with this heritage, and to expect them to go to the original sources is quite unrealistic. What we have tried to do, therefore, is to produce an anthology that can be conveniently read by student and layperson alike, that will help open some of the multiple windows of perception and illuminate some of the myriad facets of our wisdom heritage.

I am grateful to Ravi Singh of Penguin India who encouraged me to produce this volume, based on a suggestion by the littérateur and member of Parliament Pavan K. Varma. I have been greatly assisted in the task of collecting material for this anthology by Aakash Chakrabarty.

Karan Singh

THE VEDANTA

NASADIYA SUKTA

*The 'Nasadiya Sukta' is part of the Rig Veda (10.129). It talks
about the origin of the universe. One cannot fail to notice the
curious observation about the One in the last line: 'He surely
knows or maybe he does not!'*

At first there was neither Being nor Nonbeing.
There was not air nor yet sky beyond.
What was its wrapping? In whose protection?
Was Water there, Unfathomable and deep?

There was no death then, nor yet deathlessness;
of night or day there was not any sign.
The One breathed without breath, by its own impulse.
Other than that was nothing else at all.

Darkness was there, all wrapped around by darkness,
and all was Water indiscriminate.
Then that which was hidden by the Void,
That One, emerging, stirring,
Through power of Ardor (Tapas), came to be.

In the beginning Love arose, which was
the primal germ cell of the mind.
The Seers, searching in their hearts with wisdom,
Discovered the connection of Being in Nonbeing.

A crosswise line cut Being from Nonbeing.
What was described above it, what below?
Bearers of seed there were and mighty forces,
Thrust from below and forward move above.

Who really knows? Who can presume to tell it?
Whence was it born? Whence issued this creation?
Even the Gods came after its emergence.
Then who can tell from whence it came to be?

That out of which creation has arisen,
Whether it held it firm or it did not,
He who surveys it in the highest heaven,
He surely knows or maybe he does not!

Rig Veda 10.129
(Translated by Raimundo Panikkar)

PRAYER FOR LONG LIFE

This hymn from the Atharva Veda divides the hundred years of human life for various functions in the world.

(1) For a hundred autumns may we see,

(2) For a hundred autumns may we live,

(3) For a hundred autumns may we know,

(4) For a hundred autumns may we rise,

(5) For a hundred autumns may we thrive,

(6) For a hundred autumns may we be,

(7) For a hundred autumns may we become,

(8) Aye, and even more than a hundred autumns.

Atharva Veda 19.67
(Translated by A.C. Bose)

HYMN TO THE EARTH

The 'Hymn to the Earth' is an ode to nature, stressing its importance in the life of human beings, and is an eloquent statement of environmental values.

(1)   Truth, Eternal Order that is great and stern,
Consecration, Austerity, Prayer and Ritual—
these uphold the Earth.
May she, Queen of what has been and will be,
make a wide world for us.

(2)   Earth which has many heights, and slopes and.
the unconfined plain that bind men together,
Earth that bears plants of various healing powers,
may she spread wide for us and thrive.

(3)   Earth, in which lie the sea, the river and other waters,
in which food and cornfields have come to be,
in which live all that breathes and that moves,
may she confer on us the finest of her yield.

(4)   Mistress of four quarters, in whom
food and cornfields have come to be,
who bears in many forms the breathing and moving life,
may she give us cattle and crops.

(5)   Earth, in which men of old before us
performed their various work,
where Devas overwhelmed the Asuras,
Earth, the home of kine, horses, birds,
may she give us magnificence and lustre.

(6)   All-sustaining, treasure-bearing, firm staying-place,
gold-breasted, home of all moving life,
Earth bears the sacred universal fire.
May Indra and Rishava give us wealth.

(7)   Earth, whom unsleeping Devas protect for ever without
erring,
may she pour on us delicious sweets,
and endow us with lustre.

(8)   Earth, which at first was in the water of the ocean,
and which sages sought with wondrous powers,
Earth whose heart was in Eternal Heaven,
wrapped in Truth, immortal,
may she give us lustre and strength
in a most exalted State.

(9)   Earth, in which the waters, common to all,
moving on all sides, flow unfailing, day and night,
may she pour on us milk in many streams,
and endow us with lustre.

(10)   Earth, which the Ashvins measured out and Vishnu
strode,
which Indra, Lord of might,
made free from foes for himself,
may she pour out milk for me—a mother to her son.

(11)   Pleasant be thy hills, O Earth,
        thy snow-clad mountains and thy woods!
        On Earth—brown, black, ruddy and multi-coloured—
        the firm Earth protected by Indra,
        on this Earth I stand, unvanquished,
        unslain, unhurt.

(12)   Set me, O Earth, amidst what is thy centre and
        thy navel,
        and vitalizing forces that emanated from thy body.
        Purify us from all sides. Earth is my mother, her son am I;
        and Parjanya my father: may he fill us
        with plenty.

(13)   Earth, on which they build up the altar,
        and various workers spin the web of Yajna,
        on which are fixed the tall, bright poles before the
        invocation;
        may she, prospering, make us prosper.

(14)   The man, O Earth, who hates us, is hostile to us,
        who threatens us by his thoughts and his weapons,
        overwhelm him, Earth, as thou hast
        done before.

(15)   Born of thee, on thee move mortal creatures;
        thou bearest them—the biped and the quadruped.
        Thine, O Earth, are the five races of men to
        whom, mortals,
        the sun as he rises spreads, with his rays,
        the light immortal.

(16)   In concert may all creatures pour out blessings!
         Endow me, Earth, with honeyed speech.

(17)   Mother of all plants,
         firm Earth upheld by Eternal Law,
         may she be ever beneficent and gracious to us
         as we tread on her.

(18)   A vast abode art thou, and mighty,
         and mighty is thy speed, thy moving and
         thy shaking;
         and mighty Indra protects thee unerring.
         May thou, O Earth, make us shine forth
         with the brightness of gold.
         Let no one hate me.

(19)   There lies the fire within the earth,
         and in plants,
         and waters carry it;
         the fire is in stone.
         There is a fire deep within men,
         a fire in the kine,
         and a fire in horses:

(20)   The same fire that burns in the heavens;
         the mid-air belongs to this Fire Divine.
         Men kindle this fire that bears the oblation
         and loves the melted butter.

(21)   May Earth, clad in her fiery mantle,
         dark-kneed,
         make me aflame;
         may she sharpen me bright.

(22)   Earth on which they offer
            Yajna and oblation to Devas
            with many decorations,
            on which mortal men live by food and drink:
            may she give us breath and life,
            may she make us long-lived.

(23)   The fragrance that rises from thee, O Earth,
            that plants and waters carry,
            and is shared by Gandharvas, by Apsarases,
            make me sweet with that.
            May no one hate me.

(24)   The fragrance that entered the lotus,
            and that the Immortals, O Earth, first brought at
            Surya's bridal,
            make me sweet with that.
            May no one hate me.

(25)   Thy fragrance that is in men and women,
            and the majesty and lustre in males,
            in the hero and the steed,
            in the wild beast and in the elephant,
            and the radiance that is in the maiden,
            unite us with these, O Earth!
            May no one hate me.

(26)   Rock, soil, stone and dust,
            Earth is held together and bound firm.
            To her my obeisance, to gold-breasted Earth.

(27)   We invoke all-supporting Earth
            on which trees, lords of forests, stand ever firm.

(28)   Rising or sitting, standing or walking,
         may we, either with our right foot or our left,
         never totter on the earth.

(29)   I call to Earth, the purifier,
         the patient Earth, growing strong through spiritual
         might.
         May we recline on thee, O Earth,
         who bearest power, plenty, our share of food and molten
         butter.

(30)   Pure may the waters flow for our bodies' cleansing.
         To those who trespass against us
         we offer an unpleasant welcome.
         I cleanse myself, O Earth, with that
         which purifies.

(31)   May those that are thy eastern regions,
         and the northern, Earth, and the southern and the
         western,
         be pleasant for me to tread upon.
         May I not stumble while I live in the world.

(32)   Do not push me from the west or from the east,
         or from the north or the south.
         Be gracious to us, O Earth. Let not those find us
         who waylay people on the road.
         Take deadly weapons far away from us.

(33)   So long as I look on thee from around, O Earth,
         with the sun as friend,
         So long, as year follows year,
         may not my vision fail.

(34)   When, lying down, O Earth,
        I turn on my right side and on my left,
        or when we lie straight on our ribs
        against thee behind us, be thou not unkind to us
        then, O Earth,
        thou who layest all to sleep.

(35)   Whatever I dig from thee, Earth,
        may that have quick growth again.
        O purifier, may we not injure thy vitals or
        thy heart.

(36)   May thy Summer, Earth, and thy Rains,
        thy Autumn, thy dewy months, thy Winter and thy
        Spring,
        may these thy seasons, Earth, that make the year,
        and day and night
        pour their abundance on us.

(37)   She, purifier, kept away from the Serpent,
        and carried the fires within her waters,
        she, Earth, having opted for Indra and not Vritra,
        drove away the God-hating Dasyus,
        and held on to Skra, the strong and mighty.

(38)   Earth on which the sacred seat and shed are built,
        and the pole is raised;
        on which Brahmanas, versed in Yajnas,
        worship in Eic and Saman hymns,
        and priests are busy so that Indra
        may drink the Soma juice;

(39)   On which, of old, world-building Rishis
         chanted the sacred words,
         and the Seven Sages prayed in session
         with sacrifice and austerity;

(40)   May that Earth grant us the wealth that we desire.
         May Bhaga give the task, and Indra come to lead
         the way.

(41)   Earth on which men sing and dance
         while uttering various words,
         where people meet in battle,
         the war-cry rises,
         the drum sounds,
         may she drive away our enemies,
         may Earth make me free from foes.

(42)   Earth on which grow food-grains—rice and barley,
         on which live the five races of men,
         our homage be to her, Parjanya's Consort,
         who mellows with the rain.

(43)   Earth in which are cities, the work of Devas,
         and fields where men are variously employed;
         Earth that bears all things in her womb,
         may the Lord of Life make her graceful for us from
         every side.

(44)   May Earth that bears treasures in secret at many
         places,
         give me her riches, gems and gold.
         May the bounteous Goddess, giving us wealth,
         give it with loving kindness.

(45)   May Earth with people who speak various tongues,
         and those who have various religious rites
         according to their places of abode,
         pour for me treasure in a thousand streams
         like a constant cow that never fails.

(46)   The snake, and the scorpion with the sharp sting,
         that, overpowered by the cold season, lie
         bewildered in the caves,
         the worm and each thing that comes to life, O
         Earth,
         and moves about with the coming on of rains,
         may these, creeping, never creep near us.
         Bless us with what is beneficent.

(47)   Thy many pathways for men to travel on
         the roads for chariots, and for wagons to pass
         through
         on which walk together both good and evil men,
         may we be masters of those, and drive out thief
         and foe.

(48)   Earth bearing the weighty also bears the foolish,
         and endures the death of both the good and the bad,
         and, being of one accord with the boar,
         she lets loose the swine to roam wildly about.

(49)   Those thy forest animals, and wild beasts of the woods—
         lions, tigers, man-eaters that prowl about,
         and the hyena, the wolf, the bear with its evil ways,
         and Rakshas,
         drive these out, O Earth, from here, away
         from us.

(50)   And, Earth, drive away from us Gandharvas,
        Apsarases, Arayas, Kimidins,
        Pisacas and all Rakshases.

(51)   Earth to which the winged bipeds fly together—
        swans, eagles, and other birds of various kinds,
        on which the wind blows strong, raising the dust,
        bending trees,
        and flame follows the blast forward
        and backward;

(52)   Earth in which Night and Day—the black and the bright
        in union—are settled,
        which is covered and canopied over by rain—
        may she establish us with bliss
        in every dear home.

(53)   Heaven, Earth and Mid-air
        have given me this wide space,
        And Agni, Surya, Apas and All-Gods
        have together endowed me with intellect.

(54)   I am victorious,
        I am called the most exalted on the earth,
        a conqueror everywhere,
        a conqueror over everything,
        I am a victor on every side.

(55)   When, O Goddess, proceeding forward,
        and extolled by Devas, thou hadst spread
        thy renown,
        then a great glory entered into thee,
        and thou madest for thyself the four quarters.

(56)   In villages, in the forest, and in the assemblies on the earth,
       in congregations and in councils, we shall speak of thee
       in lovely terms.

(57)   As a horse scatters dust, so did Earth, since she was born,
       scatter the people who dwelt on the land,
       and she joyously sped on, the world's protectress,
       supporter of forest trees and plants.

(58)   What I speak, I speak with sweetness;
       what I look at endears itself to me;
       and I am fiery and impetuous: others who fly at me
       with wrath
       I smite down.

(59)   Peaceful, sweet-smelling, gracious, filled with milk,
       and bearing nectar in her breast,
       may Earth give with the milk her blessings to me.

(60)   With oblation Visvakarman sought her
       who had entered the light in the mid-air's ocean,
       And the delicious vessel hidden in mystery
       became manifest for the nurture of those
       who found in her their Mother.

(61)   Thou art the vessel, the Mother of the people,
       the fulfiller of wishes, far-extending.
       Whatever is wanting in thee is filled
       by Prajapati, the first-born of Eternal Order.

(62)   May those born of thee, O Earth,
       be, for our welfare, free from sickness and waste.

Wakeful through a long life, we shall become
bearers of tribute to thee.

(63)   Earth, my Mother! Set me securely with bliss
in full accord with Heaven. Wise One,
uphold me in grace and splendour.

Atharva Veda 12.1
(Translated by A.C. Bose)

ISA UPANISHAD

The Isa Upanishad, though a short text, is considered most significant for its deliberations on the nature of the Supreme Being.

> *All this is full. All that is full.*
> *From fullness, fullness comes.*
> *When fullness is taken from fullness,*
> *Fullness still remains.*

Om shanti shanti shanti

(1)   The Lord is enshrined in the hearts of all.
      The Lord is the supreme Reality.
      Rejoice in him through renunciation.
      Covet nothing. All belongs to the Lord.

(2)   Thus working may you live a hundred years.
      Thus alone will you work in real freedom.

(3)   Those who deny the Self are born again
      Blind to the Self, enveloped in darkness,
      Utterly devoid of love for the Lord.

(4)   The Self is one. Ever still, the Self is
      Swifter than thought, swifter than the senses.
      Though motionless, he outruns all pursuit.
      Without the Self, never could life exist.

(5)   The Self seems to move, but is ever still.
        He seems far away, but is ever near.
        He is within all, and he transcends all.

(6)   Those who see all creatures in themselves
        And themselves in all creatures know no fear.

(7)   Those who see all creatures in themselves
        And themselves in all creatures know no grief.
        How can the multiplicity of life
        Delude the one who sees its unity?

(8)   The Self is everywhere. Bright is the Self,
        Indivisible, untouched by sin, wise,
        Immanent and transcendent.
        He it is Who holds the cosmos together.

(9–11) In dark night live those for whom
        The world without alone is real; in night
        Darker still, for whom the world within
        Alone is real. The first leads to a life
        Of action, the second to a life of meditation.
        But those who combine action with meditation
        Cross the sea of death through action
        And enter into immortality
        Through the practice of meditation.
        So have we heard from the wise.

(12–14) In dark night live those for whom the Lord
        Is transcendent only; in night darker still,
        For whom he is immanent only.
        But those for whom he is transcendent
        And immanent cross the sea of death

With the immanent and enter into
Immortality with the transcendent.
So have we heard from the wise.

(15)   The face of truth is hidden by your orb
Of gold, O sun. May you remove your orb
So that I, who adore the true, may see

(16)   The glory of truth. O nourishing sun,
Solitary traveller, controller,
Source of life for all creatures, spread your light
And subdue your dazzling splendour
So that I may see your blessed Self.
Even that very Self am I!

(17)   May my life merge in the Immortal
When my body is reduced to ashes.
O mind, meditate on the eternal Brahman.
Remember the deeds of the past.
Remember, O mind, remember.

(18)   O God of Fire, lead us by the good path
To eternal joy. You know all our deeds.
Deliver us from evil, we who bow
And pray again and again.

Om shanti shanti shanti
(Translated by Eknath Easwaran)

CHANDOGYA UPANISHAD

*The Chandogya Upanishad is one of the oldest and primary
Upanishads. 'The Wisdom of Shandilya' reveals the observations
of the famous ascetic Shandilya. 'The Story of Satyakama' speaks
of the Brahmagyan, while Uddalaka teaches his son Shvetaketu,
the oneness of Tat Tvam Asi (thou art that).*

III

THE WISDOM OF SHANDILYA

(14.1) This universe comes forth from Brahman and will
return to Brahman. Verily, all is Brahman.

A person is what his deep desire is. It is our deepest
desire in this life that shapes the life to come. So let
us direct our deepest desires to realize the Self.

(14.2) The Self, who can be realized by the pure in heart, who
is life, light, truth, space, who gives rise to all works,
all desires, all odours, all tastes, who is beyond words,
who is joy

(14.3) abiding—this is the Self dwelling in my heart.

Smaller than a grain of rice, smaller than a grain of
barley, smaller than a mustard seed, smaller than a grain
of millet, smaller even than the kernel of a gram of
millet is the Self. This is the Self dwelling in my heart,
greater than the earth, greater than the sky, greater
than all the worlds.

(14.4) This Self who gives rise to all works, all desires, all odours, all tastes, who pervades the universe, who is beyond words, who is joy abiding, who is ever present in my heart, is Brahman indeed. To him I shall return when my ego dies.

So said Shandilya; so said Shandilya.

IV

THE STORY OF SATYAKAMA

(4.1) 'Mother,' Satyakama said, 'I feel the time has come for me to go to the home of a spiritual teacher. From whom does our family come, so that I may tell him when he asks my lineage?'

(4.2) 'I do not know, dear,' she replied. 'You were born when I was young and going from place to place as a servant. Your name is Satyakama and my name is Jabala; why not call yourself Satyakama Jabala?'

(4.3) Satyakama went to Haridrumata Gautama and said to him, 'Sir, I want to become your disciple.'

(4.4) 'What family are you from, bright one?'
'Sir, I don't know. My mother says she bore me in her youth and doesn't know my ancestry. She says that since my name is Satyakama and hers is Jabala I should call myself Satyakama Jabala.'

(4.5) 'None but a true brahmin could have said that. Fetch the firewood, my boy; I will initiate you. You have not flinched from the truth.'

He selected four hundred lean and sickly cows and gave them to Satyakama to care for. 'I shall not return,' the boy said to himself, 'until they become a thousand.'

(5.1) For years Satyakama dwelt in the forest, tending the herd. Then one day the bull of the herd said to him: 'Satyakama!'

'Sir?' he replied.

'We have become a thousand. Let us now rejoin our teacher's family, and I will tell

(5.2) you one of the four feet of Brahman.'

'Please tell me, revered sir,' the boy said.

'There are four quarters: east, west, south, and north. This is one foot of Brahman, called the Shining. To meditate on these four is to become full of light and master the resplendent regions of the cosmos, knowing this

(6.1) portion of the truth. Agni, fire, will tell you more.'

The next day Satyakama set out for his teacher's house with the herd. Towards evening he made a fire, penned the cows and

(6.2) sat by the fire facing east. The fire spoke: 'Satyakama!'

'Sir?'

'Friend, I can teach you another foot of Brahman.'

'Please do, revered sir.'

'There are four quarters: earth, sky, heaven and ocean. This is one foot of Brahman, called Without End. Know this, meditate on this reality, and your life will be without end on

(7.1) this earth. A swan will tell you more.'

The next day Satyakama drove the cows onward. Towards evening he lit a fire, penned the cows and sat by the fire facing east.

(7.2)   Then a swan flew near and said: 'Satyakama!'
        'Sir?'

(7.3)   'Friend, I can teach you another foot of Brahman.'

        'Please do, revered sir.'

        'There are four quarters: fire, the sun, the moon and lightning. These make one foot of
(7.4)   Brahman, called Full of Light. To meditate on this fourfold foot of truth is to be filled with light in this world and master the
(8.1)   world of light. A diver bird will tell you more.'
        The next day Satyakama drove the cows onward. Towards evening he lit a fire, penned
(8.2)   the cows and sat by the fire facing east. Then a diver bird flew near and spoke to him: 'Satyakama!'

        'Sir?'

(8.3)   'Friend, I can teach you another foot of Brahman.'

        'Please do, revered sir.'

        'There are four parts: breath, eye, ear and mind. This is one foot of Brahman, called
(8.4)   Established. To meditate on this fourfold foot of Brahman is to be at home in this world and master space. Whoever knows this four fold foot of Brahman is called Established.'

(9.1)   So Satyakama returned to his teacher's

(9.2)   home. 'Satyakama,' his teacher called, 'you glow like one
        who has known the truth. Tell me, who has taught you?'
        Satyakama replied, 'No human, sir. But I

(9.3)   wish to hear the truth from you alone. For I have heard
        that only the teacher's wisdom comes to fruition for
        us.'
        Then his teacher taught Satyakama that same wisdom.
        Nothing was left out from it; nothing was left out.

VI

THE STORY OF SHVETAKETU

(1.1)   Shvetaketu was Uddalaka's son.
        When he was twelve, his father said to him:
        'It is time for you to find a teacher,
        Dear one, for no one in our family
        Is a stranger to the spiritual life.'

(1.2)   So Shvetaketu went to a teacher
        And studied all the Vedas for twelve years.
        At the end of this time he returned home,
        Proud of his intellectual knowledge.
        'You seem to be proud of all this learning,'

        Said Uddalaka, 'But did you ask
        Your teacher for that spiritual wisdom

(1.3)   Which enables you to hear the unheard,
        Think the unthought, and know the unknown?'
        'What is that wisdom, Father?' asked the son.

Uddalaka said to Shvetaketu:

(1.4)   'As by knowing one lump of clay, dear one,
         We come to know all things made out of clay:
         That they differ only in name and form,
         While the stuff of which all are made is clay;

(1.5)   As by knowing one gold nugget, dear one,
         We come to know all things made out of gold:
         That they differ only in name and form,
         While the stuff of which all are made is gold;

(1.6)   As by knowing one tool of iron, dear one,
         We come to know all things made out of iron:
         That they differ only in name and form,
         While the stuff of which all are made is iron
         So through that spiritual wisdom, dear one,
         We come to know that all of life is one.'

(1.7)   'My teachers must not have known this wisdom',
         Said Shvetaketu, 'for if they had known,
         How could they have failed to teach it to me?
         Father, please instruct me in this wisdom.'

         'Yes, dear one, I will,' replied his father.

(2.2)   'In the beginning was only Being,
         One without a second.

(2.3)   Out of himself he brought forth the cosmos
         And entered into everything in it.
         There is nothing that does not come from him.
         Of everything he is the inmost Self.
         He is the truth; he is the Self supreme.
         You are that, Shvetaketu; you are that.'

'Please, Father, tell me more about this
Self.'
'Yes, dear one, I will,' Uddalaka said.

(8.1)   'Let us start with sleep.
        What happens in it?
        When a man is absorbed in dreamless sleep,
        He is one with the Self, though he knows it not.
        We say he sleeps, but he sleeps in the Self.

(8.2)   As a tethered bird grows tired of flying
        About in vain to find a place of rest
        And settles down at last on its own perch,
        So the mind, tired of wandering about
        Hither and thither, settles down at last in the
        Self, dear one, to which it is bound.

(8.4)   All creatures, dear one, have their source in him.
        He is their home; he is their strength.

(8.6)   When a man departs from this world, dear one,
        Speech merges in mind, mind in prana,
        Prana in fire, and fire in pure Being.

(8. 7) There is nothing that does not come from him.
        Of everything he is the inmost Self.
        He is the truth; he is the Self supreme.
        You are that, Shvetaketu; you are that.'

        'Please, Father, tell me more about this Self.'
        'Yes, dear one, I will,' Uddalaka said.

(9.1)   'As bees suck nectar from many a flower

(9.2)   And make their honey one, so that no drop
         Can say, "I am from this flower or that"
         All creatures, though one, know not they are that
         One.

(9.3)   There is nothing that does not come from him.
         Of everything he is the inmost Self.
         He is the truth; he is the Self supreme.
         You are that, Shvetaketu; you are that.'

         'Please tell me, Father, more about this Self.'
         'Yes, dear one, I will,' Uddalaka said.

(10. 1) 'As the rivers flowing east and west
         Merge in the sea and become one with it,
         Forgetting they were ever separate rivers,

(10.2)   So do all creatures lose their separateness
         When they merge at last into pure Being.

(10.3)   There is nothing that does not come from him.
         Of everything he is the inmost Self.
         He is the truth; he is the Self supreme.
         You are that, Shvetaketu; you are that.'

         'Please, Father, tell me more about this Self.'
         'Yes, dear one, I will,' Uddalaka said.

(11.1)   'Strike at the root of a tree; it would bleed
         But still live. Strike at the trunk; it would bleed
         But still live. Strike again at the top;
         It would bleed but still live.

The Self as life supports the tree, which stands firm
and enjoys
The nourishment it receives.

(11.2) If the Self leaves one branch, that branch withers.
        If it leaves a second, that too withers.
        If it leaves a third, that again withers.
        Let it leave the whole tree, the whole tree dies.

(11.3) Just so, dear one, when death comes and the
        Self departs from the body, the body dies.
        But the Self dies not.

        There is nothing that does not come from him.
        Of everything he is the inmost Self.
        He is the truth; he is the Self supreme.
        You are that, Shvetaketu; you are that.'
        'Please, Father, tell me more about this Self.'
        'Yes, dear one, I will,' Uddalaka said.

(12.1) 'Bring me a fruit from the nyagrodha tree.'
        'Here it is, sir.'
        'Break it. What do you see?'
        'These seeds, Father, all exceedingly small.'
        'Break one. What do you see?'
        'Nothing at all.'

(12.2) 'That hidden essence you do not see, dear one,
        From that a whole nyagrodha tree will grow.

(12.3) There is nothing that does not come from him.
        Of everything he is the inmost Self.
        He is the truth; he is the Self supreme.

You are that, Shvetaketu; you are that.'
'Please, Father, tell me more about this Self.'
'Yes, dear one, I will,' Uddalaka said.

(13.1) 'Place this salt in water and bring it here
Tomorrow morning.' The boy did.
'Where is that salt?' his father asked.

'I do not see it.'

(13.2) 'Sip here. How does it taste?'
'Salty, Father.'
'And here? And there?'
'I taste salt everywhere.'
'It is everywhere, though we see it not
Just so, dear one, the Self is everywhere,
Within all things, although we see him not.

(13.3) There is nothing that does not come from him.
Of everything he is the inmost Self.
He is truth; he is the Self supreme
You are that, Shvetaketu; you are that.'
'Please, Father, tell me more about this Self.'
'Yes, dear one, I will,' Uddalaka said.

(14.1) 'As a man from Gandhara, blindfolded,
Led away and left in a lonely place
Turns to the east and west and north and south
And shouts, "I am left here and cannot see!"

(14.2) Until one removes his blindfold and says,
"There lies Gandhara; follow that path,"
And thus informed, able to see for himself,

The man inquires from village to village
And reaches his homeland at last—just so,
My son, one who finds an illumined teacher
Attains spiritual wisdom in the Self.

(14.3) There is nothing that does not come from him.
Of everything he is the inmost Self.
He is the truth; he is the Self supreme.
You are that, Shvetaketu; you are that.'
'Please, Father, tell me more about this Self.'

(15.1) 'When a man is dying, his family
All gather round and ask,
"Do you know me? Do you know me?" And so long
as his speech
Has not merged in mind, his mind in prana,
Prana in fire, and fire in pure Being,

(15.2) He knows them all. But there is no more knowing
When speech merges in mind, mind in prana,
Prana in fire, and fire in pure Being.

(15.3) There is nothing that does not come from him.
Of everything he is the inmost Self.
He is the truth; he is the Self supreme.
You are that, Shvetaketu; you are that.'

(16.3) Then Shvetaketu understood this teaching;
Truly he understood it all.

(Translated by Eknath Easwaran)

SHVETASHVATARA UPANISHAD

This Upanishad was attributed to a sage called Shvetashvatara. It is one of the earliest expositions of Shaivism which elevates Lord Shiva to the status of the Supreme Being, at once transcendent with cosmological functions.

(1)   What is the cause of the cosmos? Is
        it Brahman?
        From where do we come? By what live?
        Where shall we find peace at last?
        What power governs the duality
        Of pleasure and pain by which we are driven?

(2)   Time, nature, necessity, accident,
        Elements, energy, intelligence—
        None of these can be the First Cause.
        They are effects, whose only purpose is
        To help the self rise above pleasure and pain.

(3)   In the depths of meditation, sages
        Saw within themselves the Lord of Love,
        Who dwells in the heart of every creature.
        Deep in the hearts of all he dwells, hidden
        Behind the gunas of law, energy,
        And inertia. He is One. He it is
        Who rules over time, space, and causality.

(4)   The world is the wheel of God, turning round
        and round with all living creatures upon its rim.

(5)   The world is the river of God,
        Flowing from him and flowing back to him.

(6)   On this ever-revolving wheel of being
        The individual self goes round and round
        Through life after life, believing itself
        To be a separate creature, until
        It sees its identity with the Lord of Love
        And attains immortality in the indivisible whole.

(7)   He is the eternal Reality, sing the scriptures,
        And the ground of existence.
        Those who perceive him in every creature
        Merge in him and are released from the wheel
        Of birth and death.

(8)   The Lord of Love holds in his hand the world,
        Composed of the changing and the changeless,
        The manifest and the unmanifest.
        The separate self, not yet aware of the Lord,
        Goes after pleasure, only to become
        Bound more and more. When it sees the Lord,
        There comes an end to its bondage.

(9)   Conscious spirit and unconscious matter
        Both have existed since the dawn of time,
        With maya appearing to connect them,
        Misrepresenting joy as outside us.

        When all these three are seen as one, the Self
        Reveals his universal form and serves
        As an instrument of the divine will.

(10)   All is change in the world of the senses,
        But changeless is the supreme Lord of Love.
        Meditate on him, be absorbed in him,
        Wake up from this dream of separateness.

(11)   Know God and all fetters will fall away.
        No longer identifying yourself
        With the body, go beyond birth and death.
        All your desires will be fulfilled in him
        Who is One without a second.

(12)   Know him to be enshrined in your heart always.
        Truly there is nothing more in life to know.
        Meditate and realize this world
        Is filled with the presence of God.

(13)   Fire is not seen until one firestick rubs
        Against another, though fire is still there,
        Hidden in the firestick. So does the Lord
        Remain hidden in the body until
        He is revealed through the mystic mantram.

(14)   Let your body be the lower firestick;
        Let the mantram be the upper. Rub them
        Against each other in meditation
        And realize the Lord.

(15)   Like oil in sesame seeds, like butter
        In cream, like water in springs, like fire
        In firesticks, so dwells the Lord of Love,
        The Self, in the very depths of consciousness.
        Realize him through truth and meditation.

(16)   The Self is hidden in the hearts of all,
         As butter lies hidden in cream. Realize
         The Self in the depths of meditation—
         The Lord of Love, supreme Reality,
         Who is the goal of all knowledge.

         This is the highest mystical teaching;
         This is the highest mystical teaching.

II

(1)   May we harness body and mind to see
         The Lord of Life, who dwells in everyone.

(2)   May we ever with one-pointed mind
         Strive for blissful union with the Lord.

(3)   May we train our senses to serve the Lord
         Through the practice of meditation.

(4)   Great is the glory of the Lord of Life,
         Infinite, omnipresent, all-knowing.
         He is known by the wise who meditate
         And conserve their vital energy.

(5)   Hear, O children of immortal bliss,
         You are born to be united with the Lord.
         Follow the path of the illumined ones
         And be united with the Lord of Life.

(6)   Kindle the fire of kundalini deep
         In meditation. Bring your mind and breath
         Under control. Drink deep of divine love,
         And you will attain the unitive state.

(7)   Dedicate yourself to the Lord of Life,
        Who is the cause of the cosmos. He will
        Remove the cause of all your suffering
        And free you from the bondage of karma.

(8)   Be seated with spinal column erect
        And turn your senses and mind deep within.
        With the mantram echoing in your heart,
        Cross over the dread sea of birth and death.

(9)   Train your senses to be obedient.
        Regulate your activities to lead you
        To the goal. Hold the reins of your mind
        As you hold the reins of restive horses.

(10)   Choose a place for meditation that is
        Clean, quiet, and cool, a cave with a smooth floor
        Without stones and dust, protected against
        Wind and rain and pleasing to the eye.

(11)   In deep meditation aspirants may
        See forms like snow or smoke. They may feel
        A strong wind blowing or a wave of heat.
        They may see within them more and more light:
        Fireflies, lightning, sun, or moon. These are signs
        That one is far on the path to Brahman.

(12–13) Health, a light body, freedom from cravings,
        A glowing skin, sonorous voice, fragrance
        Of body: these signs indicate progress
        In the practice of meditation.

(14)   Those who attain the supreme goal of life,
Realizing the Self and passing beyond
All sorrow, shine bright as a mirror
Which has been cleansed of dust.

(15)   In the supreme climax of samadhi
They realize the presence of the Lord
Within their heart. Freed from impurities,
They pass forever beyond birth and death.

(16)   The Lord dwells in the womb of the cosmos,
The creator who is in all creatures.
He is that which is born and to be born;
His face is everywhere.

(17)   Let us adore the Lord of Life, who is
Present in fire and water, plants and trees.
Let us adore the Lord of Life!
Let us adore the Lord of Life!

III

(1)   Brahman, attributeless Reality,
Becomes the Lord of Love who casts his net
Of appearance over the cosmos and rules
It from within through his divine power.
He was before creation; he will be
After dissolution. He alone is.
Those who know him become immortal.

(2)   The Lord of Love is one. There is indeed
No other. He is the inner ruler

In all beings. He projects the cosmos
From himself, maintains and withdraws it
Back into himself at the end of time.

(3)   His eyes, mouths, arms and feet are everywhere.
Projecting the cosmos out of himself,
He holds it together.

(4)   He is the source of all the powers of life.
He is the lord of all, the great seer
Who dwells forever in the cosmic womb.
May he purify our consciousness!

(5)   O Lord, in whom alone we can find peace,
May we see your divine Self and be freed
From all impure thoughts and all fear.

(6)   O Lord, from whom we receive the mantram
As a weapon to destroy our self-will,
Reveal yourself, protector of all.

(7)   You are the supreme Brahman, infinite,
Yet hidden in the hearts of all creatures.
You pervade everything. Realizing you,
We attain immortality.

(8)   I have realized the Lord of Love,
Who is the sun that dispels our darkness.
Those who realize him go beyond death;
No other way is there to immortality.

(9)   There is nothing higher than him, nothing other
Than him. His infinity is beyond great

And small. In his own glory rooted,
He stands and fills the cosmos.

(10)   He fills the cosmos, yet he transcends it.
       Those who know him leave all separateness,
       Sorrow and death behind. Those who know him not
       Live but to suffer.

(11)   The Lord of Love, omnipresent, dwelling
       In the heart of every living creature,
       All mercy, turns every face to himself.

(12)   He is the supreme Lord, who through his grace
       Moves us to seek him in our own hearts.
       He is the light that shines forever.

(13)   He is the inner Self of all,
       Hidden like a little flame in the heart.
       Only by the stilled mind can he be known.
       Those who realize him become immortal.

                            (Translated by Eknath Easwaran)

MUNDAKA UPANISHAD

*Though written in the form of mantras, the object of the
Mundaka Upanishad is to teach the knowledge of the Brahman,
which cannot be attained by sacrifices or worship, but only by
studying the Upanishads. Once the principal thought of this
Upanishad is understood all illusions fall away.*

Om, O worshipful Ones, may our ears hear that which is
auspicious, may we, well versed in the sacrifice, see with our
eyes that which is auspicious. May we, singing your praise, enjoy
our allotted span of life with strong limbs and healthy bodies.

May Indra, extolled in the scriptures, Pusah, the all-knowing,
Tarksya, who protects us from harm and Brihaspati, who
protects our spiritual lustre, grant us prosperity and further
our welfare.

Om, Peace, Peace, Peace.

Om, Brahma, the creator of the universe, the protector of the
world, arose before all the gods. He taught the knowledge of
Brahman, which is the foundation of all knowledge, to his eldest
son Atharvan. That knowledge Atharvan imparted in ancient times
to Angir. He in turn taught it to Satyawaha, son of Bharadvaja,
and the son of Bharadvaja passed it on to Angiras, the science
thus descending from the greater to the lesser sages.

Saunaka, the renowned householder, once approached
Angiras with reverence in the manner laid down by the
scriptures, and asked: 'Venerable sir, what is that, knowing
which, everything becomes known?' To him Angiras replied:
'The knowers of Brahman declare that there are two kinds of

knowledge to be acquired—the higher as well as the lower. Of these the lower consists of the Rig Veda, the Yajur Veda, the Sama Veda, the Atharva Veda, phonetics, ritual, grammar, etymology, metrics and astrology. And the higher is that by which the Imperishable is attained.

'That which is invisible, ungraspable, without origin or attributes, which has neither eyes nor ears, hands nor feet; which is eternal and many-splendoured, all-pervading and exceedingly subtle, that Imperishable Being is what the wise perceive everywhere as the source of creation.

'As the spider sends forth and gathers in (its web), as herbs sprout upon the face of the earth, as hair grows upon the head and body of man, so, from the Immutable, springs forth the universe.

'By concentrated meditation Brahman expands; from Him matter is born, from matter life, mind, truth and immortality through works. From Brahman, the all-seeing, the all-knowing, whose energy consists of infinite wisdom, from Him is born Brahma, matter, name and form.

'This is the truth; the rituals which the seers beheld in the sacred hymns are elaborated in the three Vedas. Ye lovers of the truth, perform them constantly, for they are your paths to the world of good deeds. When the sacred fire is well kindled and the flames begin to move, offer your oblations with faith between the two portions of fire.

'For those whose fire sacrifice is not accompanied by the rites to be performed at the new moon and the full moon, at the four months of rain and at the first harvest, which is without guests and without offerings to all the gods, or which is performed contrary to scriptural injunctions; for such their hopes are destroyed in all the seven worlds.

'The Black, the Fierce, the Swift-as-mind, the Crimson, the Smoke-hued, the Scintillating, the Many-splendoured—these are the seven swaying tongues of the fire. Whoever performs the rites and makes the offerings into these shining flames at the proper time, these in the form of the rays of the sun lead to where the lord of the gods resides.

'The radiant ones cry, "Come with us, come with us", as they carry him up on the rays of the sun. They speak pleasant words of sweetness and honour, saying, "This is the holy world of Brahma gained by your good works."

'Verily, frail are these rafts of the eighteen sacrificial forms, which represent only the inferior work. The ignorant who acclaim them as the highest good fall repeatedly into the domain of old age and death. Though they consider themselves to be wise and learned, they are fools wandering aimlessly like the blind led by the blind.

'Revelling in multifarious ignorance, such people think they have achieved the goal of life. But being bound to passions and attachment they do not attain knowledge and sink down in misery when the effects of their good deeds are exhausted. Such bewildered minds regard sacrifices and good works as most important, and do not know any greater good. Having reaped in heaven their rewards of good deeds they enter again this world or even a lower one.

'But those who live in the forest leading a life of austerity and faith, tranquil, wise and keeping the mendicant's rule, they, purged of all impurities, go by the solar gate to where the immutable, imperishable Being dwells.

'Having examined the worlds gained by deeds, the wise seeker should become indifferent to them, for the Eternal cannot be attained by works. To know that let him approach with humility a Guru who is learned in the scriptures and established in the Brahman. To such a seeker, whose mind is tranquil and senses controlled, and who has approached him in the proper manner, let the learned Guru impart the science of Brahman through which the true, Imperishable Being is realized.

'This is the truth. As from a blazing fire thousands of fiery sparks leap out, just so, my beloved, a multitude of beings issue forth from the Imperishable and, verily, fall back into it again.

'The divine Being is formless, eternal and pure, pervading within and without, anterior both to life and mind. He transcends even the highest immutable. From him are born life, mind and the senses; ether, air, fire, water and the all-supporting earth. Fire is his head, the sun and moon his eyes, space his ears, the Vedas his speech, the wind his breath, the universe his heart. From his feet the earth has originated; verily he is the inner self of all beings.

'From Him comes the fire fuelled by the sun; from the moon the rains which nourish herbs upon the earth. (Nourished by them) the male casts his seed into the female; thus are these many beings born of the divine Being. From Him are born the hymns of the Rig, Sama and Yajur Vedas; the sacrificial chants and the sacrifice; the ceremonies and the sacrificial gifts; the time of the sacrifice, the sacrificer and the worlds purified by the moon and illuminated by the sun.

'From Him are born the many gods and celestial beings; men, beasts and birds, the in-drawn breath and the out-breath; rice and barley; austerity and faith, truth, chastity and the law. From Him also are born the seven senses; the seven flames and their fuel, the seven oblations and the seven worlds in which move the life-breaths, seven and seven which dwell in the secret place of the heart.

'From Him are all these mountains and the oceans; from Him the multifarious rivers flow; from Him also are all the herbs and juices which, together with the elements, support the inner soul. Verily, that great Being is all this universe—sacrificial works, austerity and knowledge. O handsome youth, he who knows this immortal Being as seated in the secret caverns of the heart cuts asunder the knot of ignorance even during this life on earth.

'The Brahman is the mighty foundation, manifesting deep in the secret caverns of the heart. In it are established all that breathe, and move and see. Know this both as being and nonbeing, as the supremely desirable, greatest and highest of beings beyond all understanding. Luminous, subtler than the subtle, the imperishable Brahman is the abode of the worlds and all their peoples. It is life, it is speech, it is mind. It is reality and immortality. O beloved one, it is this which must be pierced; know it.

'Having taken a bow the great weapon of the secret Teaching, one should fix in it the arrow sharpened by constant meditation. Drawing it with a mind filled with That (Brahman), Penetrate, O good-looking youth, that Imperishable as the mark. The Pranava (Om) is the bow; the arrow is the self; Brahman is said to be the mark. With heedfulness is it to be penetrated, should become one with it as the arrow in the mark.

'He in whom are woven the sky, the earth and interspace, along with mind and all the life-breaths, know him as the one self and desist from other utterances. This is the bridge to immortality. Where all the nerves and arteries come together like the spokes of a chariot wheel at its hub, there, moving within the heart, he becomes manifold. Meditate on that self as Om; may your passage to the other shore beyond the darkness be pleasant and auspicious.

'The omniscient, the all-wise, whose glory is reflected here on earth, is the self enthroned in the luminous city of Brahman, his ethereal heaven. Firmly established in mind, seated in the heart, he controls life and body. The wise by the higher knowledge see him clearly as the radiant blissful, immortal.

'When the Great Being is seen as both the higher and the lower, the knot of the heart is rent asunder, all doubts are dispelled and Karma is destroyed. In the highest golden sheath dwells the Brahman—stainless and indivisible. He is the light of all lights; it is he that the knowers of the self realize.

'There the sun does not shine, nor the moon and the stars; there these lightnings do not shine, how then this earthly fire? Verily everything shines only after his shining; his shining illuminates this entire cosmos. Verily the immortal Brahman is everywhere; in front and behind, to the north and the south, above and below, verily Brahman alone is this great universe.

'Two beautiful birds, closely bound in friendship, cling to a common tree. Of these one eats the delicious fruit with relish, while the other looks on without eating. Seated on the same tree one of them—the personal self—grieves on account of its helplessness. But when he sees the other—the worshipful lord in all his glory—his sorrow passes away from him.

'When the seer sees the golden-hued Lord, the Great Being who is the maker of the world and the source of Brahma the creator, then the wise one, shaking off good and evil, free from stain, attains unity with the supreme. Verily it is the divine spirit that shines forth in all beings. Knowing this, the wise one desists from unnecessary talk. Sporting in the self, delighting in the self, yet involved in outer activity, such a one is the greatest among the knowers of Brahman.

'The Self within the body, pure and resplendent is attained through the cultivation of truth, austerity, right knowledge and chastity. When their impurities dwindle, the ascetics behold him. Truth alone triumphs, not untruth. By truth is laid out the divine path along which sages, their desires fulfilled, ascend to where Truth has its supreme abode.

'Vast, divine, beyond all thought processes shines the Brahman; subtler than the subtle, farther than the farthest. Yet it is nearer than the nearest, and the seer sees it within the secret heart. He cannot be grasped by the eye, by speech nor by the other sense organs. Nor can he be revealed by penance and austerities. Only when the mind becomes calm and purified by the grace of the higher knowledge does one, meditating, behold the great, indivisible Being.

'The subtle Atman within the body, pervaded by the fivefold life-force, is to be known by thought. The mind is constantly pervaded by the senses; when it is purified, the self shines forth. Whatever world the man of purified mind desires, whatever desires he wishes to fulfil, all these he attains. Therefore let whoever is desirous of prosperity worship the man of self-realization.

'The man of self-realization knows the supreme Brahman upon which the universe is based and shines radiantly. The wise, free from desire, worship the Brahman past beyond the seed of rebirth. Whoever in his mind longs for the objects of desire is born again and again for their fulfilment; but one whose desire for the Brahman is fully satisfied, for such a perfected soul all his desires vanish even here in this life.

'Not by discourses, nor by intellectual analysis, nor through much learning can the Atman be attained. He is attained only by one whom he chooses; to such a one the Atman reveals its own form. This self cannot be attained by one without strength, nor by the careless, nor through improper austerities. But the wise who strive by all these means enter into the abode of Brahman.

'Having attained the Self the seers are fully satisfied with wisdom, perfect in their souls, non-attached and tranquil. Having realized the all-pervasive everywhere, these disciplined souls verily enter into the Brahman. Firmly established in the Vedantic wisdom through the yoga of renunciation, their consciousness purified, these seers at the end of time achieve immortality and liberation in the world of Brahman.

'Gone are the fifteen parts into their foundations; the senses into the corresponding deities; the deeds and the intellect into the supreme, immutable Being. As flowing rivers disappear into the ocean, losing their separate name and form, even so the seer, freed from name and form, becomes one with the effulgent Being, the highest of the high.

'Verily, he who knows the supreme Brahman himself becomes Brahman. In his lineage none is born who knows not the Brahman. He crosses beyond sorrow; he crosses beyond sin. Liberated from the knots of the heart he becomes immortal.

'This very doctrine is declared in the Vedic verse. To them alone who perform the rites, who are well versed in the scriptures, who are firmly grounded in the Brahman, who tend the sacred fire with devotion, who have duly performed the rite of the head, should this knowledge of the Brahman be imparted. This is the truth imparted to his disciples in ancient times by the seer Angiras. Let no one who has not performed the rite study this.

'Salutations to the great seers
Salutations to the great seers.'

(Translated by Karan Singh)

THE GREAT REVOLTS

JAIN TEXTS

Jainism derives its name from the Sanskrit and Pali word 'jina', meaning 'victor'. A Jain is a follower of Jinas, who have conquered the illusion of birth and death and rediscovered 'Dharma'. They are also known as Tirthankars. The last of the twenty-four Tirthankars, 'Mahavira' Vardhamana, established the central tenets of Jainism: non-violence, truthfulness, non-stealing, chastity, non-attachment. Breaking barriers of caste he organized his followers as monks (sadhus), nuns (sadhvis), laymen (shravaks) and laywomen (shravikas). This order is known as Chaturvidh Jain Sangh.

Of Human Bondage

One should know what binds the soul, and, knowing, break free from bondage.

What bondage did the Hero declare, and what knowledge did he teach to remove it?

He who grasps at even a little, whether living or lifeless, or consents to another doing so, will never be freed from sorrow.

If a man kills living things, or slays by the hand of another, or consents to another slaying, his sin goes on increasing.

The man who cares for his kin and companions is a fool who suffers much, for their numbers are ever increasing.

All his wealth and relations cannot save him from sorrow. Only if he knows the nature of life, will he get rid of karma.

Sutrakritanga 1.1.1.1–5
(Translated by Hermann Jacobi)

Creatures Great and Small

Earth and water, fire and wind,
Grass, trees, and plants, and all creatures that move,
Born of the egg, born of the womb,
Born of dung, born of liquids—
These are the classes of living beings.
Know that they all seek happiness.
In hurting them men hurt themselves,
And will be born again among them . . .
Some men leave mother and father for the life of a monk,
But still make use of fire;
But He has said, 'Their principles are base
Who hurt for their own pleasure.'
The man who lights a fire kills living things,
While he who puts it out kills the fire;
Thus a wise man who understands the Law
Should never light a fire.
There are lives in earth and lives in water,
Hopping insects leap into the fire,
And worms dwell in rotten wood.
All are burned when a fire is lighted.
Even plants are beings, capable of growth,
Their bodies need food, they are individuals.

The reckless cut them for their own pleasure
And slay many living things in doing so.
He who carelessly destroys plants, whether sprouted
or full grown,
Provides a rod for his own back.
He has said, 'Their principles are ignoble
Who harm plants for their own pleasure.'

Sutrakritanga 1.1–9

(Translated by Hermann Jacobi)

The Hero of Penance and Self-Control

Oh man, refrain from evil, for life must come to an end.
Only men foolish and uncontrolled are plunged in the
habit of pleasure.
Live in striving and self-control, for hard to cross are
paths full of insects.
Follow the rule that the Heroes have surely proclaimed.
Heroes detached and strenuous, subduing anger and fear,
Will never kill living beings, but cease from sin and happy.
'Not I alone am the sufferer—all things in the universe
suffer!'
Thus should man think and be patient, not giving way
to his passions.
As old plaster flakes from a wall, a monk should make
thin his body by fasting,
And he should injure nothing. This is the Law taught
by the Sage.

Sutrakritanga, 1.2.1.10–14

(Translated by Hermann Jacobi)

Moral Verses

(118)   The path of virtue, like milk, is one;
        The sects that teach it are manifold.

(122)   Those who snare and keep encaged the partridge or
        the quail,
        Which dwell in the wilds where beetles hum around
        the flowers,
        Shall (in a later life) till black and hungry soil,
        Their legs in fetters, as slaves to alien lords.

(134)   Learning is a treasure that needs no safeguard;
        Nowhere can fire destroy it or proud kings take it.
        Learning's the best legacy a man can leave his
        children.
        Other things are not true wealth.

(137)   In the city of the gods, in the after-life,
        We shall learn if there is any greater joy
        Than that when wise men, with minds as keen as
        steel,
        Meet together in smiling fellowship.

(156)   You may bite the sugarcane, break its joints,
        Crush out its juice, and still it is sweet.
        Well-born men, though others abuse or hurt them
        Never lose their self-respect in words of anger.

(170)   The greatness of the great is humility.
        The gain of the gainer is self-control.

Only those rich men are truly wealthy
Who relieve the need of their neighbours.

(195)   People speak of high birth and low—
        Mere words, with no real meaning!
        Not property or ancient glory makes a man noble,
        But self-denial, wisdom and energy.

(202)   This is the duty of a true man—
        To shelter all, as a tree from the fierce sun,
        And to labour that many may enjoy what he earns,
        As the fruit of a fertile tree.

(219)   Better hatred than the friendship of fools.
        Better death than chronic illness.
        Better to be killed than soul-destroying contempt.
        Better abuse than praise undeserved.

(238)   If I do not stretch out my hand and risk my life
        For a friend in need,
        May I reap the reward of one who seduces the wife
        of a friend,
        While the wide world mocks me in scorn.

(365)   Best is a life passed in penance,
        Middling, that spent with those one loves,
        Worst, the life of one never satisfied,
        Clinging to rich men who care nothing for him.

(386)   As a scroll read by one who well understands it,
        As wealth to the man of generous spirit,

As a sharp sword in the warrior's hand,
Is the beauty of a faithful wife.

The Four Hundred Quatrains
(Translated by G.U. Pope)

BUDDHIST TEXTS

Buddhism is largely based on the teachings of Siddhartha Gautama, known as the 'Buddha', the enlightened one. He is believed to have lived between the sixth and fourth centuries BC. After attaining Nirvana, the Buddha laid down the Four Noble Truths: life as we know it leads to suffering; suffering is caused by craving; suffering ends when craving ends; and liberation can be achieved by the path laid out by the Buddha.

The Four Noble Truths

Nagasena, a Brahmin who became a Buddhist sage, lived around 150 BC. In Milinda Panha he answers questions about Buddhism posed by Menander I (Milinda in the Pali language), the Indo-Greek king of north-western India.

Thus I have heard. Once the Lord was at Varanasi, at the deer park called Isipatana. There he addressed the five monks:

'There are two ends not to be served by a wanderer. What are these two? The pursuit of desires and of the pleasure which springs from desire, which is base, common, leading to rebirth, ignoble and unprofitable; and the pursuit of pain and hardship, which is grievous, ignoble and unprofitable. The Middle Way of the Tathagata avoids both these ends. It is enlightened, it brings clear vision, it makes for wisdom, and leads to peace, insight, enlightenment and Nirvana. What is the Middle Way? . . . It is the Noble Eightfold Path—Right Views, Right Resolve, Right Speech, Right Conduct, Right Livelihood,

Right Effort, Right Mindfulness and Right Concentration. This is the Middle Way.

'And this is the Noble Truth of Sorrow. Birth is sorrow, age is sorrow, disease is sorrow, death is sorrow; contact with the unpleasant is sorrow, separation from the pleasant is sorrow, every wish unfulfilled is sorrow—in short all the five components of individuality are sorrow.

'And this is the Noble Truth of the Arising of Sorrow. It arises from craving, which leads to rebirth, which brings delight and passion, and seeks pleasure now here, now there—the craving for sensual pleasure, the craving for continued life, the craving for power.

'And this is the Noble Truth of the Stopping of Sorrow. It is the complete stopping of that craving, so that no passion remains, leaving it, being emancipated from it, being released from it, giving no place to it.

'And this is the Noble Truth of the Way which leads to the Stopping of Sorrow. It is the Noble Eightfold Path—Right Views, Right Resolve, Right Speech, Right Conduct, Right Livelihood, Right Effort, Right Mindfulness and Right Concentration.'

The Simile of the Chariot

Then King Menander went up to the Venerable Nagasena, greeted him respectfully and sat down. Nagasena replied to the greeting and the King was pleased at heart. Then King Menander asked: 'How is your reverence known, and what is your name?'

'I'm known as Nagasena, Your Majesty, that's what my fellow monks call me. But though my parents may have given me such a name . . . it's only a generally understood term, a practical designation. There is no question of a permanent individual implied in the use of the word.'

'Listen, you five hundred Greeks and eighty thousand monks!' said King Menander. 'This Nagasena has just declared that there's no permanent individuality implied in his name!' Then, turning to Nagasena, 'If, Reverend Nagasena, there is no permanent individuality, who gives you monks your robes and food, lodging and medicines? And who makes use of them? Who lives a life of righteousness, meditates, and reaches Nirvana? Who destroys living beings, steals, fornicates, tells lies or drinks spirits? . . . If what you say is true there's neither merit nor demerit, and no fruit or result of good or evil deeds. If someone were to kill you there would be no question of murder. And there would be no masters or teachers in the [Buddhist] Order and no ordinations. If your fellow monks call you Nagasena, what then is Nagasena? Would you say that your hair is Nagasena?'

'No, Your Majesty.'

'Or your nails, teeth, skin or other parts of your body, or the outward form, or sensation, or perception, or the psychic constructions, or consciousness? Are any of these Nagasena?'

'No, Your Majesty.'

'Then are all these taken together Nagasena?'

'No, Your Majesty.'

'Or anything other than they?'

'No, Your Majesty.'

'Then for all my asking I find no Nagasena. Nagasena is a mere sound! Surely what your Reverence has said is false!'

Then the Venerable Nagasena addressed the King.

'Your Majesty, how did you come here—on foot, or in a vehicle?'

'In a chariot.'

'Then tell me what is the chariot? Is the pole the chariot?'

'No, Your Reverence.'

'Or the axle, wheels, frame, reins, yoke, spokes or goad?'
'None of these things is the chariot.'

'Then all these separate parts taken together are the chariot?'
'No, Your Reverence.'

'Then is the chariot something other than the separate parts?'

'No, Your Reverence.'

'Then for all my asking, Your Majesty, I can find no chariot. The chariot is a mere sound. What then is the chariot? Surely what Your Majesty has said is false! There is no chariot!'

When he had spoken the five hundred Greeks cried, 'Well done!' and said to the King; 'Now, Your Majesty, get out of that dilemma if you can!'

'What I said was not false,' replied the King. 'It's on account of all these various components, the pole, axle, wheels, and so on, that the vehicle is called a chariot. It's just a generally understood term, a practical designation.'

'Well said, Your Majesty! You know what the word 'chariot' means! And it's just the same with me. It's on account of the various components of my being that I'm known by the generally understood term, the practical designation Nagasena.'

Milinda Panha
(Translated by Trenckner)

Right Mindfulness

The Lord was staying at Savatthi at the monastery of Anathapindaka in the Grove of Jeta. One morning he dressed, took his robe and bowl, and went into Savatthi for alms, with the Reverend Rahula following close behind him. As they walked the Lord, without looking round, spoke to him thus:

'All material forms, past, present or future, within or without, gross or subtle, base or fine, far or near, all should be viewed with full understanding—with the thought "This is not mine, this is not I, this is not my soul."'

'Only material forms, Lord?'

'No, not only material forms, Rahula, but also sensation, perception, the psychic constructions and consciousness.'

'Who would go to the village to collect alms today, when he has been exhorted by the Lord himself?' said Rahula. And he turned back and sat cross-legged, with body erect, collected in thought.

Then the Venerable Sariputta, seeing him thus, said to him: 'Develop concentration on inhalation and exhalation, for when this is developed and increased it is very productive and helpful.'

Towards evening Rahula rose and went to the Lord, and asked him how he could develop concentration on inhalation and exhalation. And the Lord said:

'Rahula, whatever is hard and solid in an individual, such as hair, nails, teeth, skin, flesh and so on, is called the personal element of earth. The personal element of water is composed of bile, phlegm, pus, blood, sweat and so on. The personal element of fire is that which warms and consumes or burns up, and produces metabolism of food and drink in digestion. The personal element of air is the wind in the body which moves upwards or downwards, the winds in the abdomen and stomach, winds which move from member to member, and the inhalation and exhalation of the breath. And finally the personal element of space comprises the orifices of ears and nose, the door of the mouth, and the channels whereby food and drink enter, remain in, and pass out of the body. These five personal elements, together with the five external elements, make up the total of the five universal elements. They should all be regarded objectively, with right understanding, thinking "This is not mine, this is not I, this is not my soul." With this understanding attitude a man turns from the five elements and his mind takes no delight in them.

'Develop a state of mind like the earth, Rahula. For on the earth men throw clean and unclean things, dung and urine, spittle, pus and blood, and the earth is not troubled or repelled or disgusted. And as you grow like the earth no contacts with pleasant or unpleasant will lay hold of your mind or stick to it. Similarly you should develop a state of mind like water, for men throw all manner of clean and unclean things into water and it is not troubled or repelled or disgusted. And similarly with fire, which burns all things, clean and unclean, and with air, which blows upon them all, and with space, which is nowhere established.

'Develop the state of mind of friendliness, Rahula, for, as you do so, ill-will will grow less; and of compassion, for thus vexation will grow less; and of joy, for thus aversion will grow less; and of equanimity, for thus repugnance will grow less.

'Develop the state of mind of consciousness of the corruption of the body, for thus passion will grow less; and of the consciousness of the fleeting nature of all things, for thus the pride of selfhood will grow less.

'Develop the state of mind of ordering the breath, in which the monk goes to the forest, or to the root of a tree or to an empty house, and sits cross-legged with body erect, collected in thought. Fully mindful he inhales and exhales. When he inhales or exhales a long breath he knows precisely that he is doing so, and similarly when inhaling or exhaling a short breath. While inhaling or exhaling he trains himself to be

conscious of the whole of his body, to be fully conscious of
the components of his mind, to realize the impermanence
of all things, or to dwell on passionlessness or renunciation.
Thus the state of ordered breathing, when developed and
increased, is very productive and helpful. And when the
mind is thus developed a man breathes his last breath in full
consciousness, and not unconsciously.'

Majjhima Nikaya, 1.420ff
(Translated by Lord Chalmers)

The Last Instructions of the Buddha

Soon after this the Lord began to recover, and when he was
quite free from sickness he came out of his lodging and sat
in its shadow on a seat spread out for him. The Venerable
Ananda went up to him, paid his respects, sat down to one
side and spoke to the Lord thus:

'I have seen the Lord in health, and I have seen the Lord
in sickness; and when I saw that the Lord was sick my body
became as weak as a creeper, my sight dimmed, and all my
faculties weakened. But yet I was a little comforted by the
thought that the Lord would not pass away until he had left
his instructions concerning the Order.'

'What, Ananda! Does the Order expect that of me? I have
taught the truth without making any distinction between
exoteric and esoteric doctrines; for ... with the Tathagata there is
no such thing as the closed fist of the teacher who keeps some
things back. If anyone thinks "It is I who will lead the Order"
or "The Order depends on me", he is the one who should lay
down instructions concerning the Order. But the Tathagata has
no such thought, so why should he leave instructions? I am
old now, Ananda, and full of years; my journey nears its end,

and I have reached my sum of days, for I am nearly eighty years old. Just as a worn-out cart can only be kept going if it is tied up with thongs, so the body of the Tathagata can only be kept going by bandaging it. Only when the Tathagata no longer attends to any outward object, when all separate sensation stops and he is deep in inner concentration, is his body at ease.

'So, Ananda, you must be your own lamps, be your own refuges. Take refuge in nothing outside yourselves. Hold firm to the truth as a lamp and a refuge, and do not look for refuge in anything besides yourselves. A monk becomes his own lamp and refuge by continually looking on his body, feelings, perceptions, moods and ideas in such a manner that he conquers the cravings and depressions of ordinary men and is always strenuous, self-possessed and collected in mind. Whoever among my monks does this, either now or when I am dead, if he is anxious to learn, will reach the summit.' [p. 99 f.]

'All composite things must pass away. Strive onward vigilantly.'

Digha Nikaya, 2.99 f.
(Translated by Rhys Davis)

The Buddha in Nirvana

'Reverend Nagasena,' said the King, 'does the Buddha still exist?'

'Yes, Your Majesty, he does.'

'Then is it possible to point out the Buddha as being here or there?'

'The Lord has passed completely away in Nirvana, so that nothing is left which could lead to the formation of another being. And so he cannot be pointed out as being here or there.'

'Give me an illustration.'

'What would Your Majesty say—if a great fire were blazing, would it be possible to point to a flame which had gone out and say that it was here or there?'

'No, Your Reverence, the flame is extinguished, it can't be detected.'

'In just the same way, Your Majesty, the Lord has passed away in Nirvana... He can only be pointed out in a body of his doctrine, for it was he who taught it.'

'Very good, Reverend Nagasena!'

(Translated by Trenckner)

Rock Edicts of Ashoka

After witnessing the bloodshed in the war of Kalinga (265–264 BC) Ashoka had a change of heart and converted to Buddhism. He set about spreading the word of Buddhism through pillar edicts throughout his vast kingdom, and sent his son Mahindra and daughter Sanghamitra to Sri Lanka. He refers to himself as 'Piyadasi', beloved of the gods, in these edicts.

RIGHT BEHAVIOUR

'Dharma is good, but what constitutes Dharma? [It includes] little evil, much good, kindness, generosity, truthfulness and purity.'

Pillar Edict Nb2

'And noble deeds of Dharma and the practice of Dharma consist of having kindness, generosity, truthfulness, purity, gentleness and goodness increase among the people.'

Rock Pillar Nb7

Ashoka showed great concern for fairness in the exercise of justice, caution and tolerance in the application of sentences, and regularly pardoned prisoners.

'It is my desire that there should be uniformity in law and uniformity in sentencing. I even go this far, to grant a three-day stay for those in prison who have been tried and sentenced to death. During this time their relatives can make appeals to have the prisoners' lives spared. If there is none to appeal on their behalf, the prisoners can give gifts in order to make merit for the next world, or observe fasts.'

Pillar Edict Nb4

'In the twenty-six years since my coronation prisoners have been given amnesty on twenty-five occasions.'

Pillar Edict Nb5

RELIGIOUS EXCHANGE

Far from being sectarian, Ashoka, based on a belief that all religions shared a common, positive essence, encouraged tolerance and understanding of other religions.

'All religions should reside everywhere, for all of them desire self-control and purity of heart.'

Rock Edict Nb7

'Here (in my domain) no living beings are to be slaughtered or offered in sacrifice.'

Rock Edict Nb1

'Contact (between religions) is good. One should listen to and respect the doctrines professed by others. Beloved-of-the-Gods, King Piyadasi, desires that all should be well learned in the good doctrines of other religions.'

Rock Edict Nb12

(Translated by S. Dhammika)

THE ACHARYAS

THE ACHARYAS

BHAGVAD GITA

The Gita is a philosophical inquiry into the human condition in the form of a dialogue between Arjuna and Lord Krishna in the Mahabharata. Responding to Arjuna's moral dilemma of fighting his cousins, Krishna explains to him his dharma. In Book X of the Gita, Krishna describes how he is the ultimate source of all material and spiritual worlds. Arjuna accepts Krishna as the Supreme Being.

Chapter X

KRISHNA

(1)   Hear again mighty Arjuna, hear the glory of my Word again. I speak for thy true good, because thy heart finds joy in me.

(2)   The hosts of the gods know not my birth, nor the great seers on earth, for all the gods come from me, and all the great seers, all.

(3)   He who knows I am beginningless, unborn, the Lord of all the worlds, this mortal is free from delusion, and from all evils he is free.

(4–5)   Intelligence, spiritual vision, victory over delusion, patient forgiveness, truth, self-harmony, peacefulness, joys and sorrows, to be and not to be, fear and freedom from fear, harmlessness and non-violence, an ever-quietness, satisfaction, simple austerity, generosity, honour and dishonour: these are conditions of mortals and they arise from me.

(6) The seven seers of times immemorial, and the four founders of the human race, being in me, came from my mind; and from them came this world of men.

(7) He who knows my glory and power, he has the oneness of unwavering harmony. This is my truth.

(8) I am the One source of all; the evolution of all comes from me. The wise think this and they worship me in love.

(9) Their thoughts are on me, their life is in me, and they give light to each other. For ever they speak of my glory; and they find peace and joy.

(10) To those who are ever in harmony, and who worship me with their love, I give the Yoga of vision and with this they come to me.

(11) In my mercy I dwell in their hearts and I dispel their darkness of ignorance by the light of the lamp of wisdom.

ARJUNA

(12) Supreme Brahman, Light supreme, and supreme purification, spirit divine eternal, unborn God from the beginning, omnipresent Lord of all.

(13) Thus all the seers praised thee: the seer divine Narada; Asita, Devala and Vyasa. And this is now thy revelation.

(14)   I have faith in all thy words, because these words are words of truth, and neither the gods in heaven nor the demons in hell can grasp thy infinite vastness.

(15)   Only thy Spirit knows thy Spirit; only thou knowest thyself. Source of Being in all beings, God of gods, ruler of all.

(16)   Tell me in thy mercy of thy divine glory wherein thou art ever, and all the worlds are.

(17)   For ever in meditation, how shall I ever know thee? And in what manifestations shall I think of thee, my lord?

(18)   Speak to me again in full of thy power and of thy glory, for I am never tired, never, of hearing thy words of life.

KRISHNA

(19)   Listen and I shall reveal to thee some manifestations of my divine glory. Only the greatest, Arjuna, for there is no end to my infinite greatness.

(20)   I am the soul, prince victorious, which dwells in the heart of all things. I am the beginning, the middle, the end of all that lives.

(21)   Among the sons of light I am Vishnu, and of luminaries the radiant sun. I am the lord of the winds and storms, and of the lights in the night I am the moon.

(22)   Of the Vedas I am the Veda of songs, and I am Indra, the chief of the gods. Above man's senses I am the mind, and in all living beings I am the light of consciousness.

(23)   Among the terrible I am the god of destruction; and among monsters Vittesa, the lord of wealth. Of radiant spirits I am fire; and among high mountains the mountain of the gods.

(24)   Of priests I am the divine priest Brihaspati, and among warriors Skanda, the god of war. Of lakes I am the vast ocean.

(25)   Among great seers I am Bhrigu; and of words I am Om, the Word of Eternity. Of prayers I am the prayer of silence; and of things that move not I am the Himalayas.

(26)   Of trees I am the tree of life, and of heavenly seers Narada. Among celestial musicians, Chitra-ratha; and among seers on earth, Kapila.

(27)   Of horses I am the horse of Indra, and of elephants his elephant Airavata. Among men I am king of men.

(28)   Of weapons I am the thunderbolt, and of cows the cow of wonder. Among creators I am the creator of love; and among serpents the serpent of Eternity.

(29)   Among the snakes of mystery I am Ananta, and of those born in the waters I am Varuna, their lord. Of the spirits of the fathers I am Aryaman, and of rulers Yama, the ruler of death.

(30)   Of demons I am Prahalada their prince, and of all things that measure I am time. Of beasts I am the king of beasts, and of birds Vainateya who carries a god.

(31)   Among things of purification I am the wind, and among
       warriors I am Rama, the hero supreme. Of fishes in the
       sea I am Makara the wonderful, and among all rivers
       the holy Ganges.

(32)   I am the beginning, the middle and the end of all that is.
       Of all knowledge I am the knowledge of the Soul. Of the
       many paths of reason I am the one that leads to Truth.

(33)   Of sounds I am the first sound, A; of compounds I am
       coordination. I am time, never-ending time. I am the
       Creator who sees all.

(34)   I am death that carries off all things, and I am the
       source of things to come. Of feminine nouns I am
       Fame and Prosperity; Speech, Memory and Intelligence;
       Constancy and patient Forgiveness.

(35)   I am the Brihat songs of all the songs in the Vedas. I
       am the Gayatri of all measures in verse. Of months I
       am the first of the year, and of seasons the season of
       flowers.

(36)   I am the cleverness in the gambler's dice. I am the
       beauty of all things beautiful. I am victory and the
       struggle for victory. I am the goodness of those who
       are good.

(37)   Of the children of Vrishni I am Krishna; and of the
       children of Pandu I am Arjuna. Among seers in silence
       I am Vyasa; and among poets the poet Usana.

(38)   I am the sceptre of the rulers of men; and I am the
         wise policy of those who seek victory. I am the silence
         of hidden mysteries; and I am the knowledge of those
         who know.

(39)   And know, Arjuna, that I am the seed of all things that
         are; and that no being that moves or moves not can
         ever be without me.

(40)   There is no end of my divine greatness, Arjuna. What
         I have spoken here to thee shows only a small part of
         my Infinity.

(41)   Know thou that whatever is beautiful and good,
         whatever has glory and power is only a portion of my
         own radiance.

(42)   But of what help is it to thee to know this diversity?
         Know that with one single fraction of my Being I
         pervade the Universe, and know that I AM.

                                   (Translated by Juan Mascaró)

KALIDASA

Kalidasa is regarded as the greatest Sanskrit poet and dramatist. Little is known about his life or the period he lived in, but legend has it that he was blessed by the goddess Saraswati, after being humiliated by his wife, and became one of the 'nine gems' at King Vikramaditya's court. 'Ritusamhara describes' the six seasons by narrating the experiences of two lovers in each of these seasons.

Ritusamhara

(1.1)   SUMMER

> The furious sun is ablaze,
> One longs for the moon,
> The pools of limpid waters
> Invite a dip evermore.
> The twilight hours are charming
> When the day dies down,
> And Cupid, churner of the mind, is weary,
> This, my love, is the advent of full Summer.

(2.1)   RAINS

> The approaching season of Rain, dear love,
> Comes like a king in pride of power,
> The rain-laden clouds are its rutting war-elephants;
> The lambent flashes of lightning
> Serve for its streaming pennons,

And the reverberating thunder
Is the rattle of its battle-drums;
It is hailed by a host of lovers
As the royal cavalcade is acclaimed
By crowds of suppliants.

(3.1)   AUTUMN

Behold! The lady Autumn comes
Clad in the silver kasa blossoms,
Her fair visage is the white lotus bloom,
The tinkling of her anklet bells is heard
In the tuneful cry of wild geese on high;
The harvest of rice with ripening sheaves,
Bending in billows in the fresh young breeze,
Is her graceful figure and supple body;
She emulates the charming bride
With white bridal vesture and lily-white face,
The jingling anklets and slender figure,
And the shoulders bowed with decorous modesty
And woman's gentle grace.

(4.13)   EARLY WINTER

Behold! The young maid, mirror in hand,
Making up her lotus face
In the sidelong morning sun;
Pouting her mouth she scans her lips
Whose essence was sucked by the lover.

(5.16)   WINTER

May this winter time
Rich in dainties, sweets and lucent syrups,
Charming with the fields of rice,

And cloying with the juice of the sugarcane,
Warm with love's awakening
And happy fulfillment,
But painful to pining lovers,
Tend to your bliss for ever!

SPRING

The trees aflower are crowned with glory,
The waters are strewn with lotus and lily,
The balmy breeze liberates fragrance,
And maidens are filled with dreams of love;
The languid perfection of the day
Wanes to a quivering twilight,
And all that breathes, or moves, or blossoms
Is sweeter, my love, in Spring.

(Translated by R.S. Pandit)

SHANKARACHARYA

Shankaracharya or Adi Shankara (AD 788–821) is considered one of the greatest exponents of Advaita Vedanta (the philosophy of non-dualism). Advaita locates the identity of the self (Atman) within the whole (Brahman). He founded four monasteries in four corners of the Indian subcontinent, which helped in the revival and spread of Vedanta. In 'Bhaja Govindam', Shankaracharya emphasizes the importance of devotion to God as a means to spiritual development and to liberation from the cycle of birth and death.

Bhaja Govindam

(4)   The water on the lotus-leaf is very unsteady; so also is life extremely unstable. Know that the entire world is devoured by disease and conceit, and struck by sorrow.

(5)   As long as you have the ability to earn money, so long will your dependants be attached to you. After that, when you live with an infirm body no one would even speak to you a word.

(6)   As long as there is breath in the body, so long will people in the household ask about one's welfare. Once the breath leaves, on the destruction of the body, the dependants dread that very same body.

(7)   When a boy, one is attached to sport; when a youth, one is attached to a young woman; when old, one is attached to anxiety; to the supreme Brahman, no one, alas, is attached!

(9)   Through the company of the good, there arises non-attachment; through non-attachment, there arises freedom from delusion; through delusionlessness, there arises steadfastness; through steadfastness, there arises liberation in life.

(10)   When youth is spent, what lustful play is there? When the water has evaporated, what lake is there? When the money is gone, what dependants are there? When the truth is known, what empirical process is there?

(11)   Do not be proud of wealth, kindred and youth; Time takes away all these in a moment. Leaving aside this entire (world) which is of the nature of an illusion, and knowing the state of Brahman, enter into it.

(12)   Day and night, dusk and dawn, winter and spring come repeatedly; Time sports, life is fleeting; yet one does not leave the winds of desire.

(14)   The ascetic with matted locks, the one with his head shaven, the one with hairs pulled out one by one, the one who disguises himself variously with the ochre-coloured robes—such a one is a fool who, though seeing, does not see. Indeed, this varied disguise is for the sake of the belly.

                                    (This verse is ascribed to Totaka.)

(15)   The body has become decrepit; the head has turned
        grey; the mouth has been rendered toothless; grasping
        a stick, the old man moves about. Even then, the mass
        of desires does not go.

                    (This verse is ascribed to Hastamalaka.)

(16)   In front, there is fire; at the back, there is the sun; in
        the night, (the ascetic sits) with the knees stuck to the
        chin; he receives alms in his palms, and lives under the
        trees; yet the bondage of desire does not leave him.

                    (This verse is ascribed to Subodha.)

(17)   One goes on pilgrimage to the place where the Ganga
        joins the sea; or observes the religious vows with care;
        or offers gifts. But if he be devoid of knowledge, he
        does not gain release—according to all schools of
        thought—even in a hundred lives.

                    (This verse is ascribed to Vaartikakara.)

(21)   Repeated birth, repeated death, and repeated lying
        in mother's womb—this transmigratory process is
        extensive and difficult to cross: save me, O Destroyer
        of Mura (O Krsna), through your grace!

                    (This verse is ascribed to Nityanatha.)

(23)   Who are you? Who am I? Whence have I come? Who
        is my mother? Who, my father? Thus inquire, leaving
        aside the entire world which is comparable to a dream,
        and is essenceless.

                    (This verse is ascribed to Surendra.)

(25)   Make no effort to be either at war with or in league
        with enemy, friend, son or relative. If you want to attain
        the status of Visnu (Godhood) soon, be equal-minded
        towards all things.

(28)   One easily takes to carnal enjoyment; afterwards, lo,
        there is disease of the body. Although, in the world,
        death is the refuge, even then one does not relinquish
        sinful ways.

(30)   The regulation of breath, the withdrawal of the senses
        (from their respective objects), the inquiry consisting
        in the discrimination between the eternal and the non-
        eternal, the method of mind-control associated with
        the muttering of mantras—perform these with great
        care.

SAIVITE SAINTS

The Saivite saints are known as the Nayanmars. Saivite devotional
poetry is collected in twelve books of Tirumurai. The first seven
books make up what are known as Tevaram (holy songs) and
are the collected works of Tirunavukkarasar (also known as
Appar), Tirugnanasambandar (Sambandar) and Sundaramurti
(Sundarar), the great three. Book 8 is given over to the works
of Manikkavasagar, another well-loved poet. The last book of
Tirumurai, Book 12, is the Periya Puranam of Sekizhar and
consists of the lives of the sixty-three canonized Saivite saints.

(1)   Those who worship you every day
       with yoghurt and milk and ghee
       don't get a penny for their devotion!
       You who live in Onakantanrali
       won't you show me a way to release
       as I wallow in this deep pit,
       dancing to the tune of the five senses,
       and won't be saved
       unless I worship your feet?

(2)   The goddess Ganga, whose waves flow
       over your moon-crowned matted hair,
       is a silent woman; Ganapati has a potbelly,
       spear-bearing Kumaran is a mere boy.
       As for the Goddess,
       she is no strict mistress.
       You who live in Onakantanrali, tell me,
       how can I serve a master with such a family?

(3)   Lord who lives in Onakantanrali,
        you won't be reasonable,
        won't take pity on the devotees
        who see you as their sole support,
        who love and worship your feet
        even when you give them nothing in return.
        What should we do in times of need,
        in poverty and misfortune—
        pawn you so that we can eat?

(4)   I have praised you, saying all I can say,
        but I can't get anything out of you.
        Onakantanrali's Lord, tell me
        how will you rule us
        when you won't give up this wretched life
        of wandering all day
        with a toothless skull for a begging bowl?

(5)   You don't grant grace to your devotees
        who dance, and sing songs to the proper beat,
        who weep and melt with love for you
        and gather to worship you in every way.
        Though I am weary, wandering about, looking for you,
        you never think of me.
        You won't run away from me, yet you won't give me
        a hand,
        Onakantanrali's Lord.

(6)   Lord who lives in Onakantanrali,
        why do you go begging for alms
        in the ancient city of Kacci with its dark woods,
        when your Goddess who has long dark hair
        and eyes curved like swords
        the mountain's daughter who wears
        the konrai garland brimming with honey

on her high breasts,
abides here in the Kamakottam shrine
for the salvation of the world?

(7)   I fritter my life away in lies
I'm neither a temple servant nor your devotee.
You have not possessed me with your truth,
nor given me hope for the future state.
Even if I were your servant,
you would ask nothing of me, give nothing,
say nothing to me!
Yet, are you not my Master from former lives,
O Lord who lives in Onakantanrali?

(8)   I hear that Death has come with his noose
to take me away,
yet I can't put strength into my heart,
can't worship your feet and be saved!
I can't join you, since I burn in this pit
of lust and envy, anger, pride and greed,
of every vice in the book, Onakantanrali's Lord!

(9)   What can your devotees who serve your holy feet
with the sacred rites get for their love?
Your necklace is a snake, you live in
Arur, a town that belongs to nobody;
Orriyur is a mortgaged city,
you have no place to call your own.
You have raised the goddess Ganga up on your head,
you've made her your wife!
Your house is the burning-ground,
and your robe the flayed hide,
O Lord who lives in Onakantanrali!

(10)   Sin will be annihilated
         for those who can sing
         this sequence of ten verses
         in which Aruran has described Onakantanrali's Lord
         who has the poet for his bondservant,
         the bull rider who is manifest as the primal syllable, 'Aum',
         and binds the colourful sari with a silken scarf
         over his loincloth.

                                   Sundarar, *Tirumurai*
                                   Book vii, hymn 5
                    (Sundarar translated by Indira Peterson)

(1)   He wears a woman's earring on one ear;
         riding on his bull,
         crowned with the pure white crescent moon,
         his body smeared with ash from the burning ground,
         he is the thief who stole my heart.
         He is the Lord who lives in fine Piramapuram,
         where he once blessed with his grace
         Brahma on the lotus seat
         who worshipped him.

(3)   He bears the white crescent moon
         on his long matted hair
         on which the river flows.
         He who makes the noisy white shell bracelets
         slip from my thin wrist,
         is the thief who stole my heart.
         He is the Lord who lives in Piramapuram,
         famed as the firstborn city of the whole world...

(5)   They praise him, calling him the Lord who is half
         woman,

Lord with the matted hair, god who rides the bull.
He is the thief who stole my heart.
He is the Lord who lives in Piramapuram,
famed as the shrine which once floated
on the dark ocean's cosmic flood.

Sambandar, *Tirumurai*
Book i, hymn 1

Aubade to Siva

Hail my life's source! Dawn is here!
With flowers to match your flower-like feet
we would worship you and await your pleasure
lit by the lovely smile of your face!
Siva, Lord of Perundurai
whose fields are cool with paddy,
both the bull ensign and I are yours—
Lord, be pleased to rise from your couch.

Aruna has reached Indra's range,
Night has fled and dawn is up
with that sun, your gracious face!
Sweet flowers blossom
and swarms of bees,
six footed, hum the sacred six syllables.
Take note, Siva, Perundurai's Lord,
Largess of Grace, Mount of Delight,
Surging Sea, rise from your couch.

The koel coos, the cock crows,
small birds twitter, conches blow;
the stars have dimmed, light in the east
gathers. Lord be pleased to reveal
your two feet, divinely decked.

Siva, Lord of Perundurai
not known to all, easy for us—
Be pleased to rise from your couch.

Sweet viol and vina players here,
chanters of Vedas and paeans there;
on one side hands with close-strung flowers
on another adorers, weepers, the faint,
palms in worship heaped over heads—
O Siva, Lord of Perundurai
who has taken even me for your slave
my Master, be pleased to rise from your couch.

You are in all elements, they say,
But unlike them, you don't come and go.
We sing and dance in praise of you
but haven't seen any who has seen you!
King of Perundurai's cool rice fields
beyond the reach of even thought,
come before us, make us whole
rule over us graciously, rise from your couch.

Your saints no longer agitated, released,
and many humans, their eyes still dim
have assembled to worship you,
Bridegroom of the wondrous maid!
Siva, Lord of Perundurai,
its red lotuses and cool fields,
snap life's bond and make us your own,
Lord be pleased to rise from your couch.

'Sweet as a fruit', 'as nectar', 'hard
to understand', 'O so easy'!
Even immortals can't size him up!
But this is his image, this Himself!

You who have thus deigned to dwell
in Uttarakosha's honeyed groves.
we shall obey the rule you lay down—
King of Perundurai, rise from your couch.

You became the First, Mid and Last,
Unknown by the Three, who else can know you?
You and your playful partner
have entered every one of our huts.
You have shown me your body, a blazing fire,
shown me your temple in Perundurai,
appeared as a Brahmin to make me your own—
Nectar unsating, arise from your couch.

O Excellence, whom the gods in heaven
cannot approach,
descended on earth that your worshippers
may adore you and live!
Sweet honey in Perundurai visible to us,
sugarcane, nectar from the sea,
the world's soul choosing our minds for your home!
Great Lord, arise from your couch.

'The days are wasted that we spend
here and not on earth,'
say Vishnu and Brahma, 'where alone
we can attain Siva.'
To please them, in your grace abounding,
be pleased to take us too for your slaves—
Nectar unsating, arise from your couch.

Manikkavasagar, *Tirupalliezhucchi*
(Manikkavachagar translated by P.S. Sundaram)

BASAVANNA

Basavanna, a social reformer of twelfth century AD, was a great philosopher, saint, economist and a champion of social equality He gave social and religious equality to women. He reformed Veerashaivism and made it the religion of the masses.

(8)   Look, the world, in a swell
of waves, is beating upon my face,

Why should it rise to my heart,
tell me,
O tell me, why is it
rising now to my throat?
Lord,
how can I tell you anything
when it is risen high
over my head
lord lord
listen to my cries
O lord of the meeting rivers
listen.

(9)   I added day by day
a digit of light
like the moon.
The python-world,
omnivorous Rahu,
devoured me.

91

Today my body
is in eclipse.
When is the release,
O lord of the meeting rivers?

(21)   Father, in my ignorance you brought me
through mothers' wombs,
through unlikely worlds.

Was it wrong just to be born,
O lord?

Have mercy on me for being born
once before.
I give you my word,
lord of the meeting rivers,
never to be born again.

(33)   Like a monkey on a tree
it leaps from branch to branch:
how can I believe or trust
this burning thing, this heart?
It will not let me go
to my Father,
my lord of the meeting rivers.

(36)   Nine hounds unleashed
on a hare,
the body's lusts
cry out:
Let go!
Let go!

Let go! Let go!
cry the lusts
of the mind.

Will my heart reach you,
O lord of the meeting rivers,

before the sensual bitches
touch and overtake?

(52)   Like a cow fallen into a quagmire
I make mouths at this corner and that,

no one to look for me
or find me

till my lord sees this beast
and lifts him out by the horns.

(59)   Cripple me, Father,
that I may not go here and there.
Blind me, Father,
that I may not look at this and that.
Deafen me, Father
that I may not hear anything else.

Keep me
at your men's feet
looking for nothing else,
O lord of the meeting rivers.

(62)   Don't make me hear all day
'Whose man, whose man, whose man is this?'

Let me hear, 'This man is mine, mine,
this man is mine.'

O lord of the meeting rivers,
make me feel I'm a son
of the house.

(64)   Siva, you have no mercy.
Siva, you have no heart.

Why why did you bring me to birth,
wretch in this world,
exile from the other?

Tell me, lord,
don't you have one more
little tree or plant
made just for me?

(70)   As a mother runs
close behind her child
with his hand on a cobra
or a fire,

the lord of the meeting rivers
stays with me
every step of the way
and looks after me.

(This poem is taken from Basavanna's
appendix to the poems.)

(97)   The master of the house, is he at home, or isn't he?
Grass on the threshold,
dirt in the house:
The master of the house, is he at home, or isn't he?

Lies in the body,
lust in the heart:
no, the master of the house is not at home,
our lord of the meeting rivers.

(99)   Does it matter how long
a rock soaks in the water:
will it ever grow soft?

Does it matter how long
I've spent in worship
when the heart is fickle?

Futile as a ghost
I stand guard over hidden gold,

O lord of the meeting rivers.

(101)   When a whore with a child
takes on a customer for money,

neither child nor lecher
will get enough of her.

She'll go pat the child once,
then go lie with the man once,

neither here nor there.
Love of money is relentless,

my lord of the meeting rivers.

(105) A snake-charmer and his noseless wife,
snake in hand, walk carefully
trying to read omens
for a son's wedding,

but they meet head-on
a noseless woman
and her snake-charming husband,
and cry 'The omens are bad!'

His own wife has no nose;
there's a snake in his hand.
What shall I call such fools
who do not know themselves

and see only the others,
O lord
of the meeting
rivers!

(111) I went to fornicate,
but all I got was counterfeit.

I went behind a ruined wall,
but scorpions stung me.

The watchman who heard my screams
just peeled off my clothes.

I went home in shame,
my husband raised weals on my back.

All the rest, O lord of the meeting rivers,
the king took for his fines.

(125)   See-saw watermills bow their heads.
So what?
Do they get to be devotees
to the Master?

The tongs join hands.
So what?
Can they be humble in service
to the Lord?

Parrots recite.
So what?
Can they read the Lord?

How can the slaves of the Bodiless God,
Desire,
know the way
our Lord's men move
or the stance of their standing?

(129)   The sacrificial lamb brought for the festival
ate up the green leaf brought for the decorations.
Not knowing a thing about the kill,
it wants only to fill its belly:
born that day, to die that day.

But tell me:
did the killers survive,
O lord of the meeting rivers?

(132)   You can make them talk
if the serpent
has stung
them.

You can make them talk
if they're struck
by an evil planet.

But you can't make them talk
if they're struck dumb
by riches.

Yet when Poverty the magician
enters, they'll speak
at once,

O lord of the meeting rivers.

(144)   The crookedness of the serpent
is straight enough for the snake-hole.

The crookedness of the river
is straight enough for the sea.

And the crookedness of our Lord's men
is straight enough for our Lord!

(161) Before
       the grey reaches the cheek,
       the wrinkle the rounded chin
       and the body becomes a cage of bones:

       before
       with fallen teeth
       and bent back
       you are someone else's ward:

       before
       you drop your hand to the knee
       and clutch a staff:

       before
       age corrodes
       your form:

       before
       death touches you:
       worship
       our lord
       of the meeting rivers!

(162) Look at them,
       busy, making an iron frame
       for a bubble on the water
       to make it safe!

       Worship the all-giving lord,
       and live
       without taking on trust
       the body's firmness.

(212)   Don't you take on
        this thing called bhakti:

        like a saw
        it cuts when it goes

        and it cuts again
        when it comes.

        If you risk your hand
        with a cobra in a pitcher
        will it let you
        pass?

(350)   a grindstone hung at the foot
        a deadwood log at the neck

        the one will not let me float
        and the other will not let me sink

        O time's true enemy
        O lord of the meeting rivers

        tide me over this life at sea
        and bring me to

            (This poem is taken from Basavanna's appendix.)

(420)   The root is the mouth
        of the tree: pour water there
        at the bottom
        and, look, it sprouts green
        at the top.

The Lord's mouth is his moving men,
feed them. The Lord will give you all.

You'll go to hell,
if, knowing they are the Lord,
you treat them as men.

(430)   Out of your eighty-four hundred thousand faces
put on just one
and come test me, ask me.

If you don't come and ask me,
I'll swear by the names of your elders.

Come in any face and ask me;
I'll give,
my lord of the meeting rivers.

(468)   I drink the water we wash your feet with,
I eat the food of worship,
and I say it's yours, everything,
goods, life, honour;
he's really the whore who takes every last bit
of her night's wages,

and will take no words
for payment,

he, my lord of the meeting rivers!

(487)   Feet will dance,
eyes will see,
tongue will sing,

and not find content,
What else, what else
shall I do?

I worship with my hands,
the heart is not content.
What else shall I do?

Listen, my lord,
it isn't enough.
I have it in me
to cleave thy belly
and enter thee

O lord of the meeting rivers!

(494)   I don't know anything like time-beats and metre
nor the arithmetic of strings and drums;
I don't know the count of iamb and dactyl

My lord of the meeting rivers,
as nothing will hurt you
I'll sing as I love.

(500)   Make of my body the beam of a lute
of my head the sounding gourd
of my nerves the strings
of my fingers the plucking rods.

Clutch me close
and play your thirty-two songs
O lord of the meeting rivers!

(555)   Certain gods
        always stand watch
        at the doors of people.
        Some will not go if you ask them to go.
        Worse than dogs, some others.
        What can they give,
        these gods,
        who live off the charity of people

        O lord of the meeting rivers?

(558)   How can I feel right
        about a god who eats up lacquer and melts,
        who wilts when he sees fire?

        How can I feel right
        about gods you sell in your need,
        and gods you bury for fear of thieves?

        The lord of the meeting rivers,
        self-born, one with himself,

        he alone is the true god.

(563)   The pot is a god. The winnowing
        fan is a god. The stone in the
        street is a god. The comb is a
        god. The bowstring is also a
        god. The bushel is a god and the
        spouted cup is a god.

        Gods, gods, there are so many
        there's no place left
        for a foot.

There is only
one god. He is our lord
of the meeting rivers.

(581)   They plunge
        wherever they see water.

        They circumambulate
        every tree they see.

        How can they know you
        O Lord
        who adore
        waters that run dry
        trees that wither?

(586)   In a Brahmin house
        where they feed the fire
        as a god

        when the fire goes wild
        and burns the house

        they splash on it
        the water of the gutter
        and the dust of the street,

        beat their breasts
        and call the crowd.

        These men then forget their worship
        and scold their fire,
        O lord of the meeting rivers!

(639)   You went riding elephants.
        You went riding horses.
        You covered yourself
        with vermilion and musk.
        O brother,
        but you went without the truth,
        you went without sowing and reaping
        the good.
        Riding rutting elephants
        of pride, you turned easy target
        to fate.
        You went without knowing
        our lord of the meeting rivers.

        You qualified for hell.

(686)   He'll grind till you're fine and small.
        He'll file till your colour shows.

        If your grain grows fine
        in the grinding,
        if you show colour
        in the filing,

        then our lord of the meeting rivers
        will love you
        and look after you.

(703)   Look here, dear fellow;
        I wear these men's clothes
        only for you.

        Sometimes I am man,
        sometimes I am woman.

O lord of the meeting rivers
I'll make wars for you
but I'll be your devotee's bride.

(705) If a rich son is born
to one born penniless,
he'll delight his father's heart
with gold counted in millions;

if a warrior son is born
to a milk-livered king
who doesn't know which way
to face a battle, he'll console
his father with a battlefront
sinking and floating
in a little sea of blood;

so will I console you
O lord of the meeting rivers,
if you should come
and ask me.

(820) The rich
will make temples for Siva.
What shall I,
a poor man,
do?

My legs are pillars,
the body the shrine,
the head a cupola
of gold.

Listen, O lord of the meeting rivers,
things standing shall fall,
but the moving ever shall stay.

(831)   I'm no worshipper;
        I'm no giver;
        I'm not even a beggar,

        O lord
        Without your grace.

        Do it all yourself, my lord of meeting rivers,
        as a mistress would
        when maids are sick.

(847)   When
        like a hailstone crystal
        like a waxwork image
        the flesh melts in pleasure
        how can I tell you?

        The waters of joy
        broke the banks
        and ran out of my eyes.

        I touched and joined
        my lord of the meeting rivers.
        How can I talk to anyone
        of that?

(848)   Sir, isn't the mind witness enough,
        for the taste on the tongue?

        Do buds wait for the garland maker's word
        to break into flower?

        Is it right, sir, to bring out the texts
        for everything?

        And, sir, is it really right to bring into the open
        the mark on our vitals
        left by our lord's love-play?

(860)   The eating bowl is not one bronze
        and the looking glass another.

        Bowl and mirror are one metal.
        Giving back light
        one becomes a mirror.

        Aware, one is the Lord's;
        unaware, a mere human.

        Worship the lord without forgetting,
        the lord of the meeting rivers.

(885)   Milk is left over
        from the calves.
        Water is left over
        from the fishes,
        flowers from the bees.

        How can I worship you,
        O Siva, with such offal?
        But it's not for me
        to despise left-overs,
        so take what comes,

        lord of the meeting rivers.

                              (Translated by A.K. Ramanujan)

TULSIDAS

Tulsidas was a great Awadhi bhakta, philosopher, composer and the author of Ramcharitmanas. Considered as one of the greatest works of mainstream Hindu literature, its composition marks the first time the story of Ramayana was made available to the common man in northern India for song and performance. In the extract in this book Vibhishana, seeing Lord Rama on foot and Ravana on a chariot, is concerned. The Lord, however, reassures him by explaining the metaphorical chariot of righteousness he rides upon.

Ramcharitmanas: Lanka Kanda (I–X)

Seeing Ravana mounted on a chariot and Raghubira on foot, Vibhishana was disconcerted. His extreme affection for the Lord made him doubtful. Respectfully, he said:

'My lord, you have no chariot nor any protection either for your body or for your feet. How, then, can you expect to conquer this stalwart hero?'

'Listen, friend,' replied the all-merciful, 'the chariot which leads one to victory is of another kind.

'Valour and fortitude are the wheels of that chariot, while truthfulness and virtuous conduct are its enduring flags and pennants; strength, discretion, self-control and benevolence are its horses, harnessed with the cords of forgiveness, compassion and equanimity.

'The worship of God is the skill of the charioteer, dispassion its shield and contentment his sword; charity is its axe and reason its lance and the highest wisdom its relentless bow.

'A pure and steady mind is its quiver, filled with the arrows of quietude, restraint and religious observances. Homage to the Brahmans and to its impenetrable buckler; there is no other way to ensure victory than this.

'He, my friend, who rides upon such a chariot of righteousness has no enemy to conquer.

'Listen, my friend; he who owns so powerful a chariot as this is a hero who can vanquish even that mighty and invincible foe: birth and death.'

(Translated by Karan Singh)

To the Formless One

AMIR KHUSRAU

Amir Khusrau (AD 1253–1325) was a musician, scholar and poet, and a spiritual disciple of Nizam ud-din Auliya. He is also known as the father of the qawwali. Though he wrote primarily in Persian, he did write a few poems in Hindavi. In his poems he addresses God as the beloved.

(1)   I am a pagan and a worshipper of love: the creed (of Muslims) I do not need;
Every vein of mine has become taut like a wire, the (Brahmin's) girdle I do not need.
Leave from my bedside, you ignorant physician!
The only cure for the patient of love is the sight of his beloved—
other than this no medicine does he need.
If there be no pilot on our boat, let there be none:
We have God in our midst: the sea we do not need.
The people of the world say that Khusrau worships idols.
So he does, so he does; the people he does not need,the world he does not need.

(Translated by Dr Hadi Hasan)

(2)   May your charming face ever shine like the full moon;
May you hold eternal sway over the domains of beauty.
By your amorous glance you have killed a poor man like me;
How magnanimous of you! May God give you a long life.
Pray do not be cruel lest you should feel ashamed of yourself

113

Before your lovers on the day of judgement.
I shall be set free from the bonds of the two worlds
If you become my companion for a while.
By your wanton playfulness you must have destroyed
Thousands of hearts of lovers like that of Khusrau.

(Translated by S.A.H. Abidi)

(3)   O you whose beautiful face is the envy of the idols of Azar
(Abraham's father and famous idol maker);
You remain superior to my praise.
All over the world have I travelled;
many a maiden's love have I tasted;
Many a beauty-star have I seen; but you are something
unique.
I have become you, and you me; I have become the body,
you the soul; So that none hereafter may say
that 'I am someone and you someone else.'
Khusrau a beggar, a stranger has come wandering to
your town;
For the sake of God, have pity on this beggar
and do not turn him away from your door.

(Translated by Dr Hadi Hasan)

(4)   The cloud weeps, and I become separated from my friend
How can I separate my heart from my heart's friend
on such a day?
The cloud weeping—and I and the friend standing,
bidding farewell—
I weeping separately, the clouds separately, the friend
separately . . .

(Translated by A. Schimmel)

KABIR

Kabir (AD 1440–1518) was a poet of the Bhakti cult. Though a Muslim, he was ordained into the Bhakti cult by the saint Ramananda. The appeal of Kabir's poems and songs lie in the use of common diction, daily metaphors and references to popular stories. His appeal to unite with the Lord is thus made accessible to one and all.

(I.13)   O servant, where dost thou seek Me?
        Lo! I am beside thee.
        I am neither in temple nor in mosque: I am neither in
        Kaaba nor in Kailash:
        Neither am I in rites and ceremonies, nor in Yoga and
        renunciation.
        If thou art a true seeker, thou shall at once see Me:
        thou shalt meet Me in a moment of time.
        Kabir says, 'O Sadhu! God is the breath of all breath.'

(I.16)   It is needless to ask of a saint the caste to which he
        belongs;
        For the priest, the warrior, the tradesman, and all the
        thirty-six castes alike are seeking for God.
        It is but folly to ask what the caste of a saint may be;
        The barber has sought God, the washerwoman and the
        carpenter—even Raidas was a seeker after God.
        The Rishi Swapacha was a tanner by caste. Hindus and
        Muslims alike have achieved that End, where remains
        no mark of distinction.

(I.22)   O brother! when I was forgetful, my true Guru showed
         me the way. Then I left off all rites and ceremonies, I
         bathed no more in the holy water:
         Then I learned that it was I alone who was mad, and the
         whole world beside me was sane; and I had disturbed
         these wise people.
         From that time forth I knew no more how to roll in
         the dust in obeisance:
         I do not ring the temple bell:
         I do not set the idol on its throne:
         I do not worship the image with flowers.
         It is not the austerities that mortify the flesh which are
         pleasing to the Lord,
         When you leave off your clothes and kill your senses,
         you do not please the Lord:
         The man who is kind and who practises righteousness,
         who remains passive amidst the affairs of the world,
         who considers all creatures on earth as his own self,
         He attains the Immortal Being, the true God is ever
         with him.
         Kabir says: 'He attains the true Name whose words are
         pure, and who is free from pride and conceit.'

(II.24) Tell me, O Swan, your ancient tale.
         From what land do you come, O Swan? To what shore
         will you fly?
         Where would you take your rest, O Swan, and what
         do you seek?
         Even this morning, O Swan, awake, arise, follow me!
         There is a land where no doubt nor sorrow have rule:
         where the terror of Death is no more.
         There the woods of spring are a-bloom, and the fragrant
         scent 'He is I' is borne on the wind:

There the bee of the heart is deeply immersed, and desires no other joy.

(II.37) O Lord Increate, who will serve Thee?
Every votary offers his worship to the God of his own creation: each day he receives service—
None seek Him, the Perfect: Brahma, the Indivisible Lord.
They believe in ten Avatars; but no Avatar can be the Infinite Spirit, for he suffers the results of his deeds:
The Supreme One must be other than this.
The Yogi, the Sannyasi, the Ascetics, are disputing one with another:
Kabir says, 'O brother! he who has seen the radiance of love, he is saved.'

(III.2) If God be within the mosque, then to whom does this world belong?
If Ram be within the image which you find upon your pilgrimage, then who is there to know what happens without?
Hari is in the East: Allah is in the West. Look within your heart, for there you will find both Karim and Ram;
All the men and women of the world are His living forms.
Kabir is the child of Allah and of Ram: He is my Guru, He is my Pir.

(Translated by Rabindranath Tagore)

SHAIKH NIZAM UD-DIN AULIYA

Shaikh Nizam ud-din Auliya (AD 1238–1325) belonged to the Chishti order of the Sufi saints. Like his predecessors, Moinuddin Chishti, Bakhtiyar Kaki and Fariduddin Ganjshakar, he stressed on love of humanity as a way of realizing God. He discouraged the demonstration of Keramat (miracles) and emphasized that it was obligatory for the Auliya (friends of God) to hide the ability of Keramat from the commoners.

The Morals of the Heart

Then he [Shaikh Nizam ud-din] said: Once upon a time there was a great man who was called Mira Kirami. A dervish wished to visit him. This dervish had the miraculous power whereby whatever he saw in a dream was correct, except for that dream which he had when the desire to see Mira Kirami seized hold of him. He set out to the place where Mira Kirami lived but along the way he halted for the night and fell asleep. In his dreams he heard that Mira Kirami had died. When daybreak came he awoke and cried: 'Alas! I have come so far to see him and he is dead. What shall I do? I will go on to the place where he was and lament at his burial place.' When he reached the locality where Mira Kirami lived, he began to ask everyone where Mira Kirami's burial place was. They replied: 'He is alive, why do you ask for his grave?' The dervish was astonished that his dream was untrue. Finally he went to see Mira Kirami and greeted him. Mira Kirami returned his greeting and said: 'Your dream was correct as to its meaning; I am usually engaged in constant recollection of God. But on the night of your dream I was occupied otherwise; therefore the cry went forth to the world that Mira Kirami had died.'

(Conversation of the Jamadi ul-Awwal, AH 708)

On Trust in God

Talk turned to trust in God. Nizam ud-din said that trust has three degrees. The first is when a man obtains a pleader for his lawsuits and this pleader is both a learned person and a friend. Then the client believes: 'I have a pleader who is both wise in presenting a suit and who is also my friend.' In this instance there is both trust and a making of requests. The client says to his lawyer: 'Answer this suit thus and bring this or that matter to such and such a conclusion.' The first stage of trust is when there is both confidence in another and the giving of instructions to another.

The second degree of trust is that of a suckling whose mother is giving milk. Here there is confidence without question. The infant does not say: 'Feed me at such and such times.' It cries but does not demand its feed [in so many words]. It does not say, 'Feed me.' It does not say, 'Give me milk.' It has confidence in its heart in its mother's compassion.

But the third degree of trust is that of a corpse in the hands of a corpse washer. It does not make requests or change or make any motion or stay quiescent [of its own volition]. As the corpse washer decides, so he turns the corpse about—and so it goes. This is the third and highest degree of trust.

(Conversation of the tenth Rabi'ul-Akhir, AH 710)

On Obedience to God

Obedience to God is of two kinds, 'intransitive' and 'transitive'. 'Intransitive' obedience is that obedience whose benefits affect only the one person—for example, prayer, fasting, pilgrimage and praising God. 'Transitive' obedience is that whose benefits and comfort reaches another. Whatever kindness in companionship and compassion is shown towards others, they call 'transitive' obedience. The rewards of this obedience are very great. There must be sincerity in 'intransitive' obedience for it to be acceptable to God. But with 'transitive' obedience, whatever one does is rewarded and acceptable to God.

(Conversation of the third Muharram, 708 AH)

On Going to Friday Prayers

A story was told that nonattendance at Friday prayers was being interpreted away (as not obligatory for a Muslim). Shaikh Nizam ud-din said there is no such interpretation. Unless someone is a captive, on a journey or ill, he who can go to Friday prayers and does not go has a very stubborn heart. Then he said, if a man does not go to one Friday congregational prayer, one black spot appears on his heart; if he misses two weeks' congregational prayer, then two black spots appear; and if he does not go three times in succession, his whole heart becomes black—which God forbid!

(Conversation of the sixth Zu'l-Hijja, 719 AH)

On The Place of the Sufi in Daily Life

Shaikh Nizam ud-din Auliya said this on the real position to be adopted about abandoning the world.

Abandoning the world is not stripping oneself naked or sitting wearing only a languta. Abandoning the world means wearing clothes and eating but not retaining what comes one's way, not acquiring anything or savouring anything, and not being attached to [worldly] things. (Conversation of the fifth Shawwal, 707 A H)

Amir Hassan Sijzi, *Fawaid ul-Fawaid*

DARA SHIKOH

Dara Shikoh (20 March 1615–30 August 1659) was the eldest son and the heir apparent of the Mughal emperor Shah Jahan and his wife Mumtaz Mahal. He was, however, defeated to the Mughal throne by his brother Aurangzeb in a bitter struggle. Known as a man of literary and philosophical pursuits Dara Shikoh espoused the coexistence of different religious traditions. One of his greatest literary projects was the translation of the Upanishads, known as Sirr-e-Akbar (The Greatest Mystery).

The Mystic Path

Here is the secret of unity (tawhid), O friend,
understand it;

Nowhere exists anything but God.
All that you see or know other than Him,
Verily is separate in name, but in essence one
with God.

Like an ocean is the essence of the Supreme Self,
Like forms in water are all souls and objects;
The ocean heaving and stirring within,
Transforms itself into drops, waves and bubbles,

So long as it does not realize its separation from
the ocean,
The drop remains a drop;

So long as he does not know himself to be the
Creator,
The created remains a created.

O you, in quest of God, you seek Him everywhere,
You verily are the God, not apart from Him!
Already in the midst of the boundless ocean,
Your quest resembles the search for a drop of the
ocean!

Dara Shikoh, *Risala-yi-Haqq-Numa*
(Translated by Bikramjeet Hasrat)

The Upanishads: God's Most Perfect Revelation

Praised be the Being, that one among whose eternal secrets is
the dot in the [letter] of the bismallah in all the heavenly books,
and glorified be the mother of books. In the holy Qur'an is the
token of His glorious name; and the angels and the heavenly
books and the prophets and the saints are all comprehended
in this name. And be the blessings of the Almighty upon the
best of His creatures, Muhammad, and upon all his children
and upon his companions universally!

To proceed: whereas this unsolicitous faqir [a religious
mendicant], Muhammad Dara Shikoh in the year 1050 after
Hijra [AD 1640] went to Kashmir, the resemblance of paradise,
and by the grace of God and the favour of the Infinite, he
there obtained the auspicious opportunity of meeting the most
perfect of the perfects, the flower of the gnostics, the tutor of
the tutors, the sage of the sages, the guide of the guides, the
unitarian accomplished in the Truth, Mulla Shah, on whom
be the peace of God. And whereas, he was impressed with a
longing to behold the gnostics of every sect, and to hear the

lofty expressions of monotheism, and had cast his eyes upon many books of mysticism and had written a number of treatises thereon, and as the thirst of investigation for unity, which is a boundless ocean, became every moment increased, subtle doubts came into his mind for which he had no possibility of solution, except by the word of the Lord and the direction of the Infinite. And whereas the holy Qur'an is mostly allegorical, and at the present day, persons thoroughly conversant with the subtleties thereof are very rare, he became desirous of bringing in view all the heavenly books, for the very words of God themselves are their own commentary; and what might be in one book compendious, in another might be found diffusive, and from the detail of one, the conciseness of the other might become comprehensible. He had, therefore, cast his eyes on the Book of Moses, the Gospels, the Psalms, and other scriptures, but the explanation of monotheism in them also was compendious and enigmatical, and from the slovenly translations which selfish persons had made, their purport was not intelligible.

Thereafter he considered as to why the discussion about monotheism is so conspicuous in India, and why the Indian theologians and mystics of the ancient school do not disavow the Unity of God nor do they find any fault with the Unitarians, but their belief is perfect in this respect; on the other hand, the ignoramuses of the present age—the highwaymen in the path of God—who have established themselves for erudites and who, falling into the traces of polemics and molestation, and apostatizing through disavowal of the true proficients in God and monotheism, display resistance against all the words of unitarianism, which are most evident from the glorious Qur'an and the authentic traditions of indubitable prophecy. And after verifications of these circumstances, it appeared that among these most ancient people, of all their heavenly books, which are the *Rig Veda*, the *Yajur Veda*, the *Sama Veda*, and the *Atharva Veda*, together with a number of ordinances, descended upon the prophets of those times, the most ancient of whom was Brahman or Adam, on whom be the peace of God, this purport is manifest from these books. And it can also be ascertained from the holy Qur'an that there is no nation without a prophet and without a revealed scripture, for it hath been said: 'Nor do We chastise until We raise an apostle' (Qur'an 17.15). And in another verse: 'And there is not a people but a warner has gone among them' (Qur'an 35.24). And at another place: 'Certainly We sent Our apostles with clear arguments, and sent down with them the Book and the measure' (Qur'an 57.25).

And the *summum bonum of* these four books, which contain all the secrets of the Path and the contemplative exercises of pure monotheism, are called the Upanekhats [Upanishads], and the people of that time have written commentaries with complete and diffusive interpretations thereon; and being still understood as the best part of their religious worship, they are always studied. And whereas this unsolicitous seeker after the Truth had in view the principle of fundamental unity of the personality and not Arabic, Syriac, Hebrew and Sanskrit languages, he wanted to make without any worldly motive, in clear style, an exact and literal translation of the Upanishad into Persian. For it is a treasure of Monotheism and there are few thoroughly conversant with it even among Indians. Thereby he also wanted to solve the mystery which underlies their efforts to conceal it from the Muslims.

And as at this period the city of Banares, which is the centre of the sciences of this community, was in certain relations with this seeker of the Truth, he assembled together the pandits and sanyasis, who were the most learned of their time and proficient in the Upanishads . . . in the year 1067 after Hijra; and thus every difficulty and sublime topic which he had desired or thought and had looked for and had not found, he obtained from these essences of the most ancient books, and without doubt or suspicion, these books are the first of all heavenly books in point of time, and source and fountainhead of all unity, in conformity with the holy Qur'an.

Happy is he, who having abandoned the prejudices of vile selfishness, sincerely and with the grace of God, renouncing all partiality, shall study and comprehend this translation entitled The Great Secret [Sirri-i-Akbar] knowing it to be a translation of the words of God. He shall become imperishable, fearless, unsolicitous, and eternally liberated.

(Translated by Bikramajeet Hasrat)

GURU NANAK

The Sikh faith was founded by Nanak (1469–1539), the first Guru
of the Sikhs. After a mystic experience in 1499, Nanak began
preaching. From Islam, Nanak took its unqualified monotheism,
rejection of idolatry and of the caste system. From Hinduism, he
borrowed the metaphysics of the Upanishads and the Gita.

Japji—The Morning Prayer

(When he compiled the Adi Granth or Granth Sahib, the fifth Guru,
Arjan Dev, gave Japji the first place in the sacred anthology. It remains
the most important prayer of the Sikhs.)

> There is One God.
> He is the supreme truth.
> He, the Creator,
> Is without fear and without hate.
> He, the Omnipresent,
> Pervades the universe.
> He is not born,
> Nor does He die to be born again.
> By His grace shalt thou worship Him.
>
> Before time itself
> There was truth.
> When time began to run its course
> He was the truth.

Even now, He is the truth
And evermore shall truth prevail.

(1)   Not by thought alone
Can He be known,
Though one thinks
A hundred thousand times;
Not in solemn silence
Nor in deep meditation.
Though fasting yields an abundance of virtue
It cannot appease the hunger for truth.
No, by none of these,
Nor by a hundred thousand other devices,
Can God be reached.
How then shall the Truth be known?
How the veil of false illusion torn?
O Nanak, thus runneth the writ divine,
The righteous path—let it be thine.

(2)   By Him are all forms created,
By Him infused with life and blessed,
By Him are some to excellence elated,
Others born lowly and depressed.
By His writ some have pleasure, others pain;
By His grace some are saved,
Others doomed to die, relive, and die again.
His will encompasseth all, there be none beside.
O Nanak, he who knows, hath no ego and no pride.

(3)   Who has the power to praise His might?
Who has the measure of His bounty?
Of His portents who has the sight?

Who can value His virtue, His deeds, His charity?
Who has the knowledge of His wisdom,
Of His deep, impenetrable thought?

How worship Him who creates life,
Then destroys,
And having destroyed doth recreate?
How worship Him who appeareth far
Yet is ever present and proximate?

There is no end to His description,
Though the speakers and their speeches be legion.

He the Giver ever giveth,
We who receive grow weary,
On His bounty humanity liveth
From primal age to posterity.

(4)   God is the Master, God is Truth,
His name spelleth love divine,
His Creatures ever cry: 'O give, O give,'
He the bounteous doth never decline.
What then in offering shall we bring
That we may see His court above?
What then shall we say in speech
That hearing may evoke His love?
In the ambrosial hours of fragrant dawn
On truth and greatness ponder in meditation,
Though action determine how thou be born,
Through grace alone cometh salvation.

O Nanak, this need we know alone,
That God and Truth are two in one.

(5)   He cannot be proved, for He is uncreated;
        He is without matter, self-existent.
        They that serve shall honoured be,
        O Nanak, the Lord is most excellent.

        Praise the Lord, hear them that do Him praise,
        In your hearts His name be graven,
        Sorrows from your soul erase
        And make your hearts a joyous haven.

        The Guru's word has the sage's wisdom,
        The Guru's word is full of learning,
        For though it be the Guru's word
        God Himself speaks therein.

        Thus run the words of the Guru:
        'God is the destroyer, preserver and creator,
        God is the Goddess too.
        Words to describe are hard to find,
        I would venture if I knew.'
        This alone my teacher taught,
        There is but one Lord of all creation,
        Forget Him not.

(8)   By hearing the word
        Men achieve wisdom, saintliness, courage and
        contentment.

        By hearing the word
        Men learn of the earth, the power that
        supports it and the firmament.

By hearing the word
Men learn of the upper and nether
regions, of islands and continents.

By hearing the word
Men conquer fear of death and the elements.

O Nanak, the word hath such magic for the worshippers,
Those that hear, death do not fear,
Their sorrows end and sins disappear.

(11)   By hearing the word
One sounds the depths of virtue's sea.

By hearing the word
One acquires learning, holiness, and royalty.

By hearing the word
The blind see and their paths are visible.

By hearing the word
The fathomless becomes fordable.

O Nanak, the word hath such magic for the worshippers,
Those that hear, death do not fear,
Their sorrows end and sins disappear.

Slok (Epilogue)

Air, water, and earth,
Of these are we made.
Air like the Guru's word gives the breath of life
To the babe born to the great mother earth

Sired by the waters.
The day and night our nurses be
That watch us in our infancy.
In their laps we play,
The world is our playground.
Our acts right and wrong at Thy court shall come
to judgment;
Some be seated near Thy seat, some ever
kept distant.
The toils have ended of those that have
worshipped Thee,
O Nanak, their faces are lit with joyful radiance, many
others they set free.

(Translated by Khushwant Singh)

GURU GOBIND SINGH

Guru Gobind Singh (1666–1708) was born in Patna, Bihar, in India and became a Guru on 11 November 1675, at the age of nine, succeeding his father Guru Tegh Bahadur. He was the leader of the Sikh faith, a warrior, a poet and a philosopher. Guru Gobind Singh's writings are collected in the Dasam Granth. Many of the last guru's hymns are used in Sikh ritual and prayer, especially the evening prayer, Rehras.

From *Akaal Ustat*

As sparks flying out of a flame
Fall back on the fire from which they rise;
As dust rising from the earth
Falls back upon the same earth;
As waves beating upon the shingle
Recede, and in the ocean mingle
So from God come all things under the sun
And to God return when their race is done.

Mitter Piyare nun, haal mureedan da kehnan

Beloved Friend, beloved God, Thou must hear
Thy servant's plight: when thou art not near
The comforts' cloak is a pall of pest,
The home is like a serpent's nest;
The wine chokes like a hangman's noose,
The rim of the goblet is an assassin's knife.

With Thee shall I in adversity dwell,
Without Thee life in ease is life in hell.

Ap hath dae mujhae ubariyae

With your own hands uplift me
From fear of death set me free;
Forever remain on my side
May your sabre and banner by me abide.

Rakhi lehu muhi rakhanhare

Protect me O great protector
Lord of saints, helper of your loved ones;
Always friend of the poor, foe of the evil remain
Lord, the fourteen worlds are within your domain.

Kal payi brahma bapu dhara

When the right time came you created Brahma the
creator
When the right time came you created Shiva the
destroyer
At the right time, you sent Vishnu the preserver;
Eternal time is your plaything forever.

Javan kal sabh jagat banayo

He who did the entire world create
Also created gods, demons and yakshas;
He is the alpha and omega of time, the only
incarnation
Understand that He is my only Guru.

Ghat ghat ke antar ki janat

The throbbing of every heart he hears
Pain of the good and wicked he knows;
From the tiny ant to the mighty elephant
He casts a benign look on all and is content.

Santan dukh paye te dukhi

When the godly suffer, He too suffers
When they are happy, He too rejoices;
The pain of those in pain He shares
The beating of every heart He hears.

Jab udakrakh kara kartara

In expansive mood the Creator did the world create
His creatures different shapes and forms did take;
Whenever He withdraws in Himself in a whim
All of them will merge in Him.

Nirankar Nribikar Nirlambh

Formless, immaculate, self-supporting
Primal, stainless, beyond time, self-born;
Only fools try to probe into His existence
Even sacred texts know not His essence.

Ekae rup anup sarupa

You are in many forms manifest
At one place you are a beggar, at another a king;
You create life from egg, womb and sweat
And from the earth many riches beget.

Kahun phul raja hae baetha

At some places you are a flower-bedecked king sitting
on his throne
At others you are a hermit shrunken to the bone;
Your creation is a display of wonderment
You were before time, through the ages, self-existent.

Khadag ket mae tihari

In the battlefield your protection I crave
Extend your hand and your servant save;
In every place be my guide and helper
From wickedness and sorrow grant me shelter.

Panyi gahe jab te tumre

Ever since I clutched your feet,
My eyes have not beheld another.
With Ram, Rahim, Puran and Koran, and others I did
not bother.
Of Simritis, Shastras, Vedas and other texts I took no
notice.
It is by virtue of your banner and your sword,
What I have written is not mine but your sacred
word.

Sagal duar kau chchadi kae

I passed by all doors before I stopped at yours
Hold me in your arms, and my honour save
Gobind will forever be your slave.

Dehra maseet soi puja au namaaz oi

He is in the temple as He is in the mosque,
He is in the Hindu worship as He is in the Muslim
prayer.
Gods and demons who guard the treasures
Of the God of riches, the musicians celestial,
The Hindus and the Muslims—they are all one.
They have each the habits of different homes,
But all men have the same eyes, the same body,
The same form compounded of the same four
elements—
Earth, air, fire and water.
Thus the Abhekh of the Hindus and the Allah of the
Muslims are one,
The Qur'an and the Puran praise the same Lord.
They are all of one form,
The one Lord made them all.

Kon bheo mundia sanyasi

One man by shaving his head
Hopes to become a holy monk,
Another sets up as a yogi
Or some other kind of ascetic.
Some call themselves Hindus
Others call themselves Mussalmans . . .
And yet man is of one race all over the world;
God as Creator, and God as Good
God in His Bounty and God in His Mercy
Is all One God. Even in our errors
We must not separate God from God!
Worship the One God,

For all men the One Divine Teacher.
All men have the same Form.
All men have the same Soul.

Naam thaam na jaat roop na rekh

He has no name, no dwelling-place, no caste;
He is the Primal Being, Gracious and Benign,
Unborn, Ever Perfect and Eternal.
He is of no nation and wears no distinguishing garb;
He has no outer likeness; He is free from Desire.
To the east or the west,
Look where you may,
He pervades and prevails
As love and affection.

From *Bicitra Natak*

For though my thoughts were lost in prayer
At the feet of Almighty God,
I was ordained to establish a sect and lay down its
rules.
But whosoever regards me as Lord
Shall be damned and destroyed.

I am—and of this let there be no doubt—
I am but the slave of God, as other men are,
A beholder of the wonders of creation.

From *Zafarnama:*

I am the destroyer of turbulent hillmen
Since they are idolaters and I am the breaker
of idols.

From *Svaiye:*

Some worship stones and on their heads bear them,
Some the phallus strung in necklaces wear its
emblem.
Some behold their god in the south, some to the west
bow their head.
Some worship images, others busy praying to the
dead.
The world is thus bound in false ritual
And God's secret is still unread.

From *Jap Sahib:*

God has no friends nor enemies.
He needs no hallelujahs nor cares about curses.
Being the first and timeless
How could He manifest Himself through these
Who are born and die?

From *Sabad Hazare*

Let thine own house be the forest
Thy heart the anchorite.
Eat little, sleep little,
Learn to love, be merciful and forbear.
Be mild, be patient,
Have no lust nor wrath,
Greed nor obstinacy.

From *Candi Caritr*

O Lord, these boons of Thee I ask,
Let me never shun a righteous task,
Let me be fearless when I go into battle,

Give me faith that victory will be mine,
Give me power to sing Thy praise,
And when comes the time to end my life,
Let me fall in mighty strife.

(Translated by Khushwant Singh)

THE MODERNS

MIRZA GHALIB

Mirza Asadullah Baig Khan (27 December 1797–15 February 1869), also known as Ghalib and Asad, was an Urdu and a Persian poet. He saw the downfall of the Mughals following the defeat of Bahadur Shah Zafar, the last Mughal king. He expanded the scope of the ghazal to include philosophical queries, which was before him an expression of anguished love. His Urdu ghazals are considered the best in the oeuvre.

(1)   *Aah ko chahiye ek umr asar hone tak*

A sigh requires a lifetime to take effect
Who lives to reach the source of your mystery

The gaping mouths of a hundred crocodiles form netted
traps in each wave
Consider the labour within the sea-change of a raindrop
to a pearl

Love demands endurance, while desire is consuming
What should be my state until obsession devours
patience

I agree that you will not remain indifferent, but
I will be dust by the time you become aware of me

The sun's ray teaches a dewdrop how to vanish
I live because you have not bestowed the grace of your
attention upon me

Leisure for life is no more than the flash of a glance,
O ignorant!
The warmth of festivity is one dance of the flame

Asad, what can cure the grief of existence, except dying.
The candle is obliged to burn before extinguishing at dawn.

(2)   *Dil hi toh hai na sang-o-khisht . . .*

It is only a heart, not stone or mortar, why should it
not fill with pain
We will wail a thousand times, why should anyone
torment us?

It is not a temple, mosque, a dearly beloved's door nor
a patron's entryway
We are wayfarers, why should anyone evict us?

The glorious beauty of that face, so much like the
midday sun
That manifests such blinding light, needs nothing like
a veil

Weaponry of seduction, arrows of untold invitation
Could injure the reflected as much as the admirer

The prison-house of life and the chains of grief, in
reality, are the same
Before perishing, why should there be any release from
suffering?

Beauty and its narcissism, ironically spare the lustful
With seduction's assurance of its power, what need to
test the rival?

There the pride of state and grace, here the ways
of courtesy
Where can we meet along the way, why should
they invite me to their assembly?

Granted they are not a lover of God, yes, they
are unfaithful
Whoever holds creed and heart beloved, do not dare
to wander up their way

Without this brittle Ghalib, what industry will
be stopped?
Why cry so incessantly, why lament so endlessly?

(3)   *Yeh na thi hamari qismat ke visaal-e-yeaar hota*
It was never in my fate to be united with
my beloved
If I had lived any longer, it would be nothing but
more waiting

Waiting with those promises that I know to
be falsities
Had I belief in them, I would have died of joy

Your fragility is such that your pledge would be
necessarily frail
Were there any parallels between us, the vow could
never be broken

Ask my heart about your half-drawn bow
This anguish would not arise had the arrow passed
through my body

What kind of friendship, my friends have turned to preaching
No one brings solutions, no one brings compassion

The veined stone has burst into an incessant flow of blood
When touched by that ember which you think is merely my grief

Grief consumes the soul; what escape from the heart's domain
If it were not the sorrows of love, there would be the sorrows of the world

To whom can I even explain, the dark night of separation
What had I against death if only it did not come again and again

Being so humiliated in death, why did I not drown instead
Then there would be no funeral, no one required to mourn at my tomb

Who can witness Him, He is singular in His Oneness
The fragrance of two, could produce encounters with many

Your mystical flights, Ghalib, your manner of expression
We would think of you as a seer, if you were not a wine lover

(Translated by Azra Raza and Sara Suleri Goodyear)

RAMMOHUN ROY

*Raja Rammohun Roy (14 August 1774–27 September 1833) was
one of the founders (along with Dwarkanath Tagore) of the
Brahma Sabha in 1828, which later became the Brahmo Samaj.
He is known for the reforms he sought to bring in Indian society,
especially his efforts to abolish the practice of sati. One of the
most important figures in the Bengal Renaissance, Rammohun
Roy, in the following extract, writes to Lord Amherst explaining
the need to educate the people of India in Western languages and
sciences.*

Letter on Education

To His Excellency the Right Honourable Lord Amherst
Governor-General in Council

My Lord,

Humbly reluctant as the natives of India are to obtrude upon
the notice of government the sentiments they entertain on any
public measure, there are circumstances when silence would be
carrying this respectful feeling to culpable excess. The present
rulers of India, coming from a distance of many thousand
miles to govern a people whose language, literature, manners,
customs and ideas are almost entirely new and strange to them,
cannot easily become so intimately acquainted with their real
circumstances as the natives of the country are themselves.
We should therefore be guilty of a gross dereliction of duty
to ourselves and afford our rulers just grounds of complaint

at our apathy did we omit, on occasions of importance like the present, to supply them with such accurate information as might enable them to devise and adopt measures calculated to be beneficial to the country, and thus second by our local knowledge and experience their declared benevolent intentions for its improvement.

The establishment of a new Sanscrit School in Calcutta evinces the laudable desire of government to improve the natives of India by education—a blessing for which they must ever be grateful, and every well-wisher of the human race must be desirous that the efforts made to promote it should be guided by the most enlightened principles, so that the stream of intelligence may flow in the most useful channels.

When this seminary of learning was proposed, we understood that the government in England had ordered a considerable sum of money to be annually devoted to the instruction of its Indian subjects. We were filled with sanguine hopes that this sum would be laid out in employing European gentlemen of talent and education to instruct the natives of India in mathematics, natural philosophy, chemistry, anatomy and other useful sciences, which the natives of Europe have carried to a degree of perfection that has raised them above the inhabitants of other parts of the world.

While we looked forward with pleasing hope to the dawn of knowledge thus promised to the rising generation, our hearts were filled with mingled feelings of delight and gratitude, we already offered up thanks to Providence for inspiring the most generous and enlightened nations of the West with the glorious ambition of planting in Asia the arts and sciences of modern Europe.

We find that the government are establishing a Sanscrit school under Hindu pandits to impart such knowledge as is already current in India. This seminary (similar in character to those which existed in Europe before the time of Lord Bacon) can only be expected to load the minds of youth with grammatical niceties and metaphysical distinctions of little or no practical use to the possessors or to society. The pupils will there acquire what was known two thousand years ago with the addition of vain and empty subtleties since then produced by speculative men such as is already commonly taught in all parts of India.

The Sanscrit language, so difficult that almost a lifetime is necessary for its acquisition, is well known to have been for ages a lamentable check to the diffusion of knowledge, and the learning concealed under this almost impervious veil is far from sufficient to reward the labour of acquiring it. But if it were thought necessary to perpetuate this language for the sake of the portion of valuable information it contains, this might be much more easily accomplished by other means than the establishment of a new Sanscrit college; for there have been always and are now numerous professors of Sanscrit in the different parts of the country engaged in teaching this language, as well as the other branches of literature which are to be the object of the new seminary. Therefore their more diligent cultivation, if desirable, would be effectually promoted, by holding out premiums and granting certain allowances to their most eminent professors, who have already undertaken on their own account to teach them, and would by such rewards be stimulated to still greater exertion.

From these considerations, as the sum set apart for the instruction of the natives of India was intended by the government in England for the improvement of its Indian subjects, I beg leave to state, with due deference to your Lordship's exalted situation, that if the plan now adopted be followed, it will completely defeat the object proposed, since no improvement can be expected from inducing young men to consume a dozen years of the most valuable period of their lives in acquiring the niceties of Vyakaran or Sanscrit grammar, for instance, in learning to discuss such points as the following: *khada,* signifying to eat, *khadati* he or she eats, query, whether does *khadati* taken as a whole convey the meaning he, she, or it eats, or are separate parts of this meaning conveyed by distinctions of the words, as if in the English language it were asked how much meaning is there in the *eat* and how much in the *s,* and is the whole meaning of the word conveyed by these two portions of it distinctly or by them taken jointly?

Neither can much improvement arise from such speculations as the following which are the themes suggested by the Vedanta: In what manner is the soul absorbed in the Deity? What relation does it bear to the Divine Essence? Nor will youths be fitted to be better members of society by the Vedantic doctrines which teach them to believe that all visible things have no real existence, that as father, brother, etc., have no real entity, they consequently deserve no real affection, and therefore the sooner we escape from them and leave the world the better.

Again, no essential benefit can be derived by the student of the Mimamsa from knowing what it is that makes the killer of a goat sinless by pronouncing certain passages of the Vedanta and what is the real nature and operative influence of passages of the Vedas, etc.

The student of the Nyaya Shastra cannot be said to have improved his mind after he has learned from it into how many ideal classes the objects in the universe are divided, and what speculative relation the soul bears to the body, the body to the soul, the eye to the ear, etc.

In order to enable your Lordship to appreciate the utility of encouraging such imaginary learning as above characterized,

I beg your Lordship will be pleased to compare the state of science and literature in Europe before the time of Lord Bacon with the progress of knowledge made since he wrote.

If it had been intended to keep the British nation in ignorance of real knowledge, the Baconian philosophy would not have been allowed to displace the system of the schoolmen which was the best calculated to perpetuate ignorance. In the same manner the Sanscrit system of education would be the best calculated to keep this country in darkness, if such had been the policy of the British legislature. But as the improvement of the native population is the object of the government, it will consequently promote a more liberal and enlightened system of instruction, embracing mathematics, natural philosophy, chemistry, anatomy, with other useful sciences, which may be accomplished with the sums proposed by employing a few gentlemen of talent and learning educated in Europe and providing a college furnished with necessary books, instruments and other apparatus.

In presenting this subject to your Lordship, I conceive myself discharging a solemn duty which I owe to my countrymen, and also to that enlightened sovereign and legislature which have extended their benevolent care to this distant land, actuated by a desire to improve the inhabitants, and therefore humbly trust you will excuse the liberty I have taken in thus expressing my sentiments to your Lordship.

I have the honour, etc.

Rammohun Roy

SWAMI VIVEKANANDA

Narendranath Dutta (12 January 1863–4 July 1902) was a Hindu monk and the chief disciple of the great nineteenth-century Indian mystic Sri Ramkrishna Paramhansa. He was instrumental in introducing and spreading the philosophy of Vedanta in the Western world. Swami Vivekananda, which means 'the bliss of discerning wisdom', made a profound impact in his speeches at the First Parliament of World Religions in Chicago in 1893.

Sisters and Brothers of America (Chicago, September 1893)

Sisters and brothers of America,

It fills my heart with joy unspeakable to rise in response to the warm and cordial welcome which you have given us. I thank you in the name of the most ancient order of monks in the world; I thank you in the name of the mother of religions; and I thank you in the name of the millions and millions of Hindu people of all classes and sects.

My thanks, also, to some of the speakers on this platform who, referring to the delegates from the Orient, have told you that these men from far-off nations may well claim the honour of bearing to different lands the idea of toleration. I am proud to belong to a religion which has taught the world both tolerance and universal acceptance. We believe not only in universal toleration, but we accept all religions as true. I am proud to belong to a nation which has sheltered the persecuted and the refugees of all religions and all nations of the earth. I am proud to tell you that we have gathered in our bosom the purest remnant of the Israelites, who came to the southern India and took refuge with us in the very year in which their holy temple was shattered to pieces by Roman tyranny. I am proud to belong to the religion which has sheltered and is still fostering the remnant of the grand Zoroastrian nation. I will quote to you, brethren, a few lines from a hymn which I remember to have repeated from my earliest boyhood, which is every day repeated by millions of human beings:

'As the different streams having their sources in different places all mingle their water in the sea, so, O Lord, the different paths which men take through different tendencies, various though they appear, crooked or straight, all lead to Thee.'

The present convention, which is one of the most august assemblies ever held, is in itself a vindication, a declaration to the world, of the wonderful doctrine preached in the Gita:

'Whosoever comes to Me, through whatsoever form, I reach him; all men are struggling through paths which in the end lead to Me.'

Sectarianism, bigotry, and its horrible descendant, fanaticism, have long possessed this beautiful earth. They have filled the earth with violence, drenched it often and often with human blood, destroyed civilization, and sent whole nations to despair. Had it not been for these horrible demons, human society would be far more advanced than it is now. But their time has come; and I fervently hope that the bell that tolled this morning in honour of this convention may be the death-knell of all fanaticism, of all persecutions with the sword or with the pen, and of all uncharitable feelings between persons wending their way to the same goal.

SRI AUROBINDO

Aurobindo Ghosh (15 August 1872–5 December 1950) was a freedom fighter and philosopher. He joined the movement for India's freedom from British rule and for a duration (1905–10), became one of its most important leaders, before turning to developing his own vision and philosophy of human progress and spiritual evolution. The central theme of Sri Aurobindo's vision is the evolution of life into a 'life divine'. In his own words: 'The step from man to superman is the next approaching achievement in the earth's evolution. It is inevitable because it is at once the intention of the inner spirit and the logic of Nature's process.'

The Hour of God

There are moments when the Spirit moves among men and the breath of the Lord is abroad upon the waters of our being; there are others when it retires and men are left to act in the strength or the weakness of their own egoism. The first are periods when even a little effort produces great results and changes destiny; the second are spaces of time when much labour goes to the making of a little result. It is true that the latter may prepare the former, may be the little smoke of sacrifice going up to heaven which calls down the rain of God's bounty.

Unhappy is the man or the nation which, when the divine moment arrives, is found sleeping or unprepared to use it, because the lamp has not been kept trimmed for the welcome and the ears are sealed to the call. But thrice woe to them who are strong and ready, yet waste the force or misuse the moment; for them is irreparable loss or a great destruction.

In the hour of God cleanse thy soul of all self-deceit and hypocrisy and vain self-flattering that thou mayst look straight into thy spirit and hear that which summons it. All insincerity of nature, once thy defence against the eye of the Master and the light of the ideal, becomes now a gap in thy armour and invites the blow. Even if thou conquer for the moment, it is the worse for thee, for the blow shall come afterwards and cast thee down in the midst of thy triumph. But being pure cast aside all fear; for the hour is often terrible, a fire and a whirlwind and a tempest, a treading of the winepress of the wrath of God; but he who can stand up in it on the truth of his purpose is he who shall stand; even though he fall, he shall rise again; even though he seem to pass on the wings of the wind, he shall return. Nor let worldly prudence whisper too closely in thy ear; for it is the hour of the unexpected, the incalculable, the immeasurable. Mete not the power of the Breath by thy petty instruments, but trust and go forward.

But most keep thy soul clear, even if for a while, of the clamour of the ego. Then shall a fire march before thee in the night and the storm be thy helper and thy flag shall wave on the highest height of the greatness that was to be conquered.

The Law of the Way

First be sure of the call and of thy soul's answer. For if the call is not true, not the touch of God's powers or the voice of his messengers, but the lure of thy ego, the end of thy endeavour will be a poor spiritual fiasco or else a deep disaster.

And if not the soul's fervour, but only the mind's assent or interest replies to the divine summons or only the lower life's desire clutches at some side attraction of the fruits of Yoga-power or Yoga-pleasure or only a transient emotion leaps like an unsteady flame moved by the intensity of the Voice or its sweetness or grandeur, then too there can be little surety for thee in the difficult path of Yoga.

The outer instruments of mortal man have no force to carry him through the severe ardours of this spiritual journey and Titanic inner battle or to meet its terrible or obstinate ordeals or nerve him to face and overcome its subtle and formidable dangers. Only his spirit's august and steadfast will and the quenchless fire of his soul's invincible ardour are sufficient for this difficult transformation and this high improbable endeavour.

Imagine not the way is easy; the way is long, arduous, dangerous, difficult. At every step is an ambush, at every turn a pitfall. A thousand seen or unseen enemies will start up against thee, terrible in subtlety against thy ignorance, formidable in power against thy weakness. And when with pain thou hast destroyed them, other thousands will surge up to take their place. Hell will vomit its hordes to oppose thee and enring and wound and menace; Heaven will meet thee with its pitiless tests and its cold luminous denials. Thou shalt find thyself alone in thy anguish, the demons furious in thy path, the Gods unwilling above thee. Ancient and powerful, cruel, unvanquished and close and innumerable are the dark and dreadful Powers that profit by the reign of Night and Ignorance and would have no change and are hostile.

Aloof, slow to arrive, far-off and few and brief in their visits are the Bright Ones who are willing or permitted to succour. Each step forward is a battle. There are precipitous descents, there are unending ascensions and ever higher peaks upon peaks to conquer. Each plateau climbed is but a stage on the way and reveals endless heights beyond it. Each victory thou thinkest the last triumphant struggle proves to be but the prelude to a hundred fierce and perilous battles . . .

But thou sayst God's hands will be with me and the Divine Mother near with her gracious smile of succour? And thou knowst not then that God's Grace is more difficult to have or to keep than the nectar of the Immortals or Kuvera's priceless treasures? Ask of his chosen and they will tell thee how often the Eternal has covered his face from them, how often he has withdrawn from them behind his mysterious veil and they have found themselves alone in the grip of Hell, solitary in the horror of the darkness, naked and defenseless in the anguish of the battle.

And if his presence is felt behind the veil, yet it is like the winter sun behind clouds and saves not from the rain and snow and the calamitous storm and the harsh wind and the bitter cold and the atmosphere of a sorrowful grey and the dun weary dullness. Doubtless the help is there even when it seems to be withdrawn, but still is there the appearance of total night with no sun to come and no star of hope to please in the darkness.

Beautiful is the face of the Divine Mother, but she too can be hard and terrible. Nay, then, is immortality a plaything to be given lightly to a child, or the divine life a prize without effort or the crown for a weakling? Strive rightly and thou shalt have; trust and thy trust shall in the end be justified; but the dread Law of the Way is there and none can abrogate it.

The Divine Superman

This is thy work and the aim of thy being and that for which thou art here, to become the divine superman and a perfect vessel of the Godhead. All else that thou hast to do, is only a making thyself ready or a joy by the way or a fall from thy purpose. But the goal is this and the purpose is this and not in power of the way and the joy by the way but in the joy of the goal is the greatness and the delight of thy being. The joy of the way is because that which is drawing thee is also with thee on thy path and the power to climb was given thee that thou mightest mount to thy own summits.

If thou hast a duty, this is thy duty; if thou ask what shall be thy aim, let this be thy aim; if thou demand pleasure, there is no greater joy, for all other joy is broken or limited, the joy of a dream or the joy of a sleep or the joy of self-forgetting. But this is the joy of thy whole being. For if thou say what is my being, this is thy being, the Divine, and all else is only its broken or its perverse appearance. If thou seek the Truth, this is the Truth. Place it before thee and in all things be faithful to it.

It has been well said by one who saw but through a veil and mistook the veil for the face, that thy aim is to become thyself; and he said well again that the nature of man is to transcend himself. This is indeed his nature and that is indeed the divine aim of his self-transcending.

What then is the self that thou hast to transcend and what is the self that thou hast to become? For it is here that thou shouldst make no error; for this error, not to know thyself, is the fountain of all thy grief and the cause of all thy stumbling.

That which thou hast to transcend is the self that thou appearest to be, and that is man as thou knowest him, the apparent Purusha. And what is this man? He is a mental being enslaved to life and matter; and where he is not enslaved to life and matter, he is the slave of his mind. But this is a great and heavy servitude; for to be the slave of mind is to be the slave of the false, the limited and the apparent.

The self that thou hast to become, is the self that thou art within behind the veil of mind and life and matter. It is to be the spiritual, the divine, the superman, the real Purusha. For that which is above the mental being, is the superman. It is to be the master of thy mind, thy life and thy body; it is to be a king over Nature of whom thou art now the tool, lifted above her who now has thee under her feet. It is to be free and not a slave, to be one and not divided, to be immortal and not obscured by death, to be full of light and not darkened, to be full of bliss and not the sport of grief and suffering, to be uplifted into power and not cast down into weakness. It is to live in the Infinite and possess the finite. It is to live in God and be one with him in his being. To become thyself is to be this and all that flows from it.

Be free in thyself, and therefore free in thy mind, free in thy life and thy body. For the Spirit is freedom.

Be one with God and all beings; live in thyself and not in thy little ego. For the Spirit is unity.

Be thyself, immortal, and put not thy faith in death; for death is not of thyself, but of thy body. For the Spirit is immortality.

To be immortal is to be infinite in being and consciousness and bliss; for the Spirit is infinite and that which is finite lives only by his infinity.

These things thou art, therefore thou canst become all these; but if thou were not these things, then thou couldst never become them. What is within thee, that alone can be revealed in thy being. Thou appearest indeed to be other than this, but wherefore shouldst thou enslave thyself to appearances?

Rather arise, transcend thyself, become thyself. Thou art man and the whole nature of man is to become more than himself. He was the man-animal, he has become more than the animal man. He is the thinker, the craftsman, the seeker after beauty. He shall be more than the thinker, he shall be the seer of knowledge; he shall be more than the craftsman, he shall be the creator and master of his creation; he shall be more than the seeker of beauty, for he shall enjoy all beauty and all delight. Physical, he seeks for his immortal substance; vital, he seeks after immortal life and the infinite power of his being; mental and partial in knowledge, he seeks after the whole light and the utter vision.

To possess these is to become the superman; for it is to rise out of mind into the supermind. Call it the divine mind or Knowledge or the supermind; it is the power and light of the divine will and the divine consciousness. By the super-mind the Spirit saw and created himself in the worlds, by that he lives in them and governs them. By that he is Swarat Samrat, self-ruler and all-ruler.

Supermind is superman; therefore to rise beyond mind is the condition.

To be the superman is to live the divine life, to be a god; for the gods are the powers of God. Be a power of God in humanity.

To live in the divine Being and let the consciousness and bliss, the will and knowledge of the Spirit possess thee and play with thee and through thee, this is the meaning.

This is the transfiguration of thyself on the mountain. It is to discover God in thyself and reveal him to thyself in all things. Live in his being, shine with his light, act with his power, rejoice with his bliss. Be that Fire and that Sun and that Ocean. Be that joy and that greatness and that beauty. When thou hast done this even in part, thou hast attained the first steps of supermanhood.

RABINDRANATH TAGORE

*Poet, novelist, musician and playwright, 'Gurudev' Rabindrath
Tagore (7 May 1861–7 August 1941) reshaped Bengali literature
and music in the late nineteenth and early twentieth centuries.
He received the Nobel Prize in 1913 for the English translation
of* Gitanjali. *He conferred the title of 'Mahatma' on Mohandas
Karamchand Gandhi.*

Where the Mind Is without Fear

Where the mind is without fear and the head is held high;
Where knowledge is free;
Where the world has not been broken up into fragments
by narrow domestic walls;
Where words come out from the depth of truth;
Where tireless striving stretches its arms towards
perfection;
Where the clear stream of reason has not lost its way
into the dreary desert sand of dead habit;
Where the mind is led forward by thee into ever-
widening thought and action—
Into that heaven of freedom, my Father, let my country
awake.

Soul Consciousness

We have seen that it was the aspiration of ancient India to
live and move and have its joy in Brahma, the all-conscious

and all pervading Spirit, by extending its field of consciousness over all the world. But that, it may be urged, is an impossible task for man to achieve. If this extension of consciousness be an outward process, then it is endless; it is like attempting to cross the ocean after ladling out its water. By beginning to try to realize all, one has to end by realizing nothing.

But, in reality, it is not so absurd as it sounds. Man has every day to solve this problem of enlarging his region and adjusting his burdens. His burdens are many, too numerous for him to carry, but he knows that by adopting a system he can lighten the weight of his load. Whenever they feel too complicated and unwieldy, he knows it is because he has not been able to hit upon the system which would have set everything in place and distributed the weight evenly. This search for system is really a search for unity, for synthesis; it is our attempt to harmonise the heterogeneous complexity of outward materials by an inner adjustment. In the search we gradually become aware that to find out the One is to possess the All; that there, indeed, is our last and highest privilege. It is based on the law of that unity which is, if we only know it, our abiding strength. Its living principle is the power that is in truth; the truth of that unity which comprehends multiplicity. Facts are many, but the truth is one. The animal intelligence knows facts, the human mind has power to apprehend truth. The apple falls from the tree, the rain descends upon the earth—you can go on burdening your memory with such facts and never come to an end. But once you get hold of the law of gravitation you can dispense with the necessity of collecting facts ad infinitum. You have got at one truth which governs numberless facts. This discovery of truth is pure joy to man—it is a liberation of his mind. For, a mere fact is like a blind lane, it leads only to itself—it has no beyond. But a truth opens up a whole horizon, it leads us to the infinite. That is the reason why, when a man like Darwin discovers some simple general truth about biology, it does not stop there, but like a lamp shedding its light far beyond the object for which it was lighted, it illumines the whole region of human life and thought, transcending its original purpose. Thus we find that truth, while investing all facts, is not a mere aggregate of facts—it surpasses them on all sides and points to the infinite reality.

As in the region of knowledge so in that of consciousness, man must clearly realize some central truth which will give him an outlook over the widest possible field. And that is the object which the Upanishad has in view when it says, 'Know thine own Soul.' Or, in other words, realize the one great principle of unity that there is in every man.

All our egoistic impulses, our selfish desires, obscure our true vision of the soul. For they only indicate our own narrow self. When we are conscious of our soul, we perceive the inner being that transcends our ego and has its deeper affinity with the All.

Children, when they begin to learn each separate letter of the alphabet, find no pleasure in it, because they miss the real purpose of the lesson; in fact, while letters claim our attention only in themselves and as isolated things, they fatigue us. They become a source of joy to us only when they combine into words and sentences and convey an idea.

Likewise, our soul when detached and imprisoned within the narrow limits of a self loses its significance. For its very essence is unity. It can only find out its truth by unifying itself with others, and only then it has its joy. Man was troubled and he lived in a state of fear so long as he had not discovered the uniformity of law in nature; till then the world was alien to him. The law that he discovered is nothing but the perception of harmony that prevails between reason which is of the soul of man and the workings of the world. This is the bond of union through which man is related to the world in which he lives, and he feels an exceeding joy when he finds this out, for then he realizes himself in his surroundings. To understand anything is to find in it something which is our own, and it is the discovery of ourselves outside us which makes us glad. This relation of understanding is partial, but the relation of love is complete. In love the sense of difference is obliterated and the human soul fulfils its purpose in perfection, transcending the limits of itself and reaching across the threshold of the infinite. Therefore love is the highest bliss that man can attain to, for through it alone he truly knows that he is more than himself, and that he is at one with the All.

This principal of unity which man has in his soul is ever active, establishing relations far and wide through literature, art, and science, society, statecraft, and religion. Our great Revealers are they who make manifest the true meaning of the soul by giving up self for the love of mankind. They face calumny and persecution, deprivation and death in their service of love. They live the life of the soul, not of the self, and thus they prove to us the ultimate truth of humanity. We call them Mahatmas, 'the men of the great soul'.

Sadhana: The Realization of Life

MOHANDAS KARAMCHAND GANDHI

Mohandas Karamchand Gandhi (2 October 1869–30 January 1948), known to Indians as Mahatma Gandhi and 'Father of the Nation', led India to independence on 15 August 1947. He used satyagraha and non-violence as his methods of achieving freedom. His teachings have influenced others around the world including Nelson Mandela and Martin Luther King, Junior.

Acquaintance with Religions

Towards the end of my second year in England I came across two Theosophists, brothers, and both unmarried. They talked to me about the Gita. They were reading Sir Edwin Arnold's translation *The Song Celestial*—and they invited me to read the original with them. I felt ashamed, as I had read the divine poem neither in Sanskrit nor in Gujarati. I was constrained to tell them that I had not read the Gita, but that I would gladly read it with them, and that though my knowledge of Sanskrit was meagre, still I hoped to be able to understand the original to the extent of telling where the translation failed to bring out the meaning. I began reading the Gita with them.

The verses in the second chapter, 'If one Ponders on objects of the sense, there springs Attraction; from attraction, grows desire, Desire flames to fierce passion, passion breeds Recklessness; then the memory—all betrayed—Lets noble purpose go, and saps the mind, Till purpose, mind, and man are all undone,' made a deep impression on my mind, and they still ring in my ears.

The book struck me as one of priceless worth. The impression has ever since been growing on me with the result that I regard it today as the book par excellence for the knowledge of Truth. It has afforded me invaluable help in my moments of gloom. I have read almost all the English translations of it, and I regard Sir Edwin Arnold's as the best. He has been faithful to the text, and yet it does not read like a translation. Though I read the Gita with these friends, I cannot pretend to have studied it then. It was only after some years that it became a book of daily reading.

The brothers also recommended *The Light of Asia* by Sir Edwin Arnold, whom I knew till then as the author only of *The Song Celestial*, and I read it with even greater interest than I did the Bhagavad Gita. Once I had begun it I could not leave off. They also took me on one occasion to the Blavatsky Lodge and introduced me to Madame Blavatsky and Mrs Besant. The latter had just then joined the Theosophical Society, and I was following with great interest the controversy about her conversion. The friends advised me to join the Society, but I politely declined saying, 'With my meagre knowledge of my own religion I do not want to belong to any religious body.' I recall having read, at the brothers' instance, Madame Blavatsky's *Key to Theosophy*. This book stimulated in me the desire to read books on Hinduism, and disabused me of the notion fostered by the missionaries that Hinduism was rife with superstition.

About the same time I met a good Christian from Manchester in a vegetarian boarding house. He talked to me about Christianity. I narrated to him my Rajkot recollections. He was pained to hear them.

He said, 'I am a vegetarian. I do not drink. Many Christians are meat-eaters and drink, no doubt; but neither meat-eating nor drinking is enjoined by Scripture. Do please read the Bible.' I accepted his advice, and he got me a copy. I have a faint recollection that he himself used to sell copies of the Bible, and I purchased from him an edition containing maps, concordance and other aids. I began reading it, but I could not possibly read through the Old Testament. I read the book of Genesis, and the chapters that followed invariably sent me to sleep. But just for the sake of being able to say that I had read it, I plodded through the other books with much difficulty and without the least interest or understanding. I disliked reading the Book of Numbers.

But the New Testament produced a different impression, especially the Sermon on the Mount which went straight to my heart. I compared it with the Gita. The verses, 'But I say unto you, that ye resist not evil: but whosoever shall smite thee on thy right cheek, turn to him the other also. And if any man take away thy coat let him have thy cloak too,' delighted me beyond measure and put me in mind of Shamal Bhatt's 'For a bowl of water, give a goodly meal' etc. My young mind tried to unify the teaching of the Gita, *The Light of Asia* and the Sermon on the Mount. That renunciation was the highest form of religion appealed to me greatly.

This reading whetted my appetite for studying the lives of other religious teachers. A friend recommended Carlyle's *Heroes and Hero-worship*. I read the chapter on the Hero as a prophet and learnt of the Prophet's greatness and bravery and austere living.

Beyond this acquaintance with religion I could not go at the moment, as reading for the examination left me scarcely any time for outside subjects. But I took mental note of the fact that I should read more religious books and acquaint myself with all the principal religions.

And how could I help knowing something of atheism too? Every Indian knew Bradlaugh's name and his so-called atheism. I read some book about it, the name of which I forget. It had no effect on me, for I had already crossed the Sahara of atheism. Mrs Besant, who was then very much in the limelight, had turned to theism from atheism, and that fact also strengthened my aversion to atheism. I had read her book *How I Became a Theosophist*.

It was about this time that Bradlaugh died. He was buried in the Woking Cemetery. I attended the funeral, as I believe every Indian residing in London did. A few clergymen also were present to do him the last honours. On our way back from the funeral we had to wait at the station for our train. A champion atheist from the crowd heckled one of these clergymen. 'Well, sir, do you believe in the existence of God?' 'I do,' said the good man in a low tone.

'You also agree that the circumference of the Earth is 28,000 miles, don't you?' said the atheist with a smile of self-assurance.

'Indeed.' 'Pray tell me then the size of your God and where he may be?' 'Well, if we but knew, He resides in the hearts of us both.' 'Now, now, don't take me to be a child,' said the champion with a triumphant look at us.

The clergyman assumed a humble silence.

This talk still further increased my prejudice against atheism.

Through Love to God

My uniform experience has convinced me that there is no other God than Truth. And if every page of these chapters does not proclaim to the reader that the only means for the realization of Truth is ahimsa, I shall deem all my labour in writing these chapters to have been in vain. And, even though my efforts in this behalf may prove fruitless, let the readers know that the vehicle, not the great principle, is at fault. After all, however sincere my strivings after ahimsa may have been, they have still been imperfect and inadequate. The little fleeting glimpses, therefore, that I have been able to have of Truth can hardly convey an idea of the indescribable lustre of Truth, a million times more intense than that of the sun we daily see with our eyes. In fact what I have caught is only the faintest glimmer of that mighty effulgence. But this much I can say with assurance, as a result of all my experiments, that a perfect vision of Truth can only follow a complete realization of ahimsa.

To see the universal and all-pervading Spirit of Truth face to face one must be able to love the meanest of creation as oneself. And a man who aspires after that cannot afford to keep out of any field of life. That is why my devotion to Truth has drawn me into the field of politics; and I can say without the slightest hesitation, and yet in all humility, that those who say that religion has nothing to do with politics do not know what religion means.

Identification with everything that lives is impossible without self-purification; without self-purification the observance of the law of ahimsa must remain an empty dream; God can never be realized by one who is not pure of heart. Self-purification therefore must mean purification in all the walks of life. And purification being highly infectious, purification of one's surroundings.

But the path of self-purification is hard and steep. To attain to perfect purity one has to become absolutely passion-free in thought, speech and action; to rise above the opposing currents of love and hatred, attachment and repulsion. I know that I have not in me as yet that triple purity, in spite of constant ceaseless striving for it. That is why the world's praise fails to move me, indeed it very often stings me. To conquer the subtle passions to me to be harder far than the physical conquest of the world by the force of arms. Ever since my return to India I have had experience of the dormant passions lying hidden with in me. The knowledge of them has made me feel humiliated though not defeated. The experiences and experiments have sustained me and given me great joy. But I know that I have still before me a difficult path to traverse. I must reduce muself to zero. So long as a man does not of his own free will put himself last among his fellow creatures, there is no salvation for him. Ahimsa is the farthest limit of humility.

In bidding farewell to the reader, for the time being at any rate, I ask him to join with me in prayer to the God of Truth that He may grant me the boon of Ahimsa in mind, word and deed.

An Autobiography or The Story of My Experiments with Truth

MUHAMMAD IQBAL

Muhammad Iqbal (9 November 1877–21 April 1938) was a poet, philosopher and politician. He is commonly referred to as Allama Iqbal in Pakistan. Iqbal was a strong proponent of the political and spiritual revival of Islamic civilization, specifically in South Asia. A series of famous lectures he delivered on this were published as The Reconstruction of Religious Thought in Islam. *Iqbal was the first to put forward the idea of a 'state in northwestern India for Muslims'.*

Muslims Are Bound Together by Faith Alone

The bond of Turk and Arab is not ours,
The link that binds us is no fetter's chain
Of ancient lineage; our hearts are bound
To the beloved Prophet of Hejaz,
And to each other are we joined through him.
Our common thread is simple loyalty
To him alone; the rapture of his wine
Alone our eyes' entrances; from what time
This glad intoxication with his love
Raced in our blood, the old is set ablaze
In new creation. As the blood that flows
Within a people's veins, so is his love
Sole substance of our solidarity.
Love dwells within the spirit, lineage
The flesh inhabits; stronger far than race
And common ancestry is love's firm cord.

True loverhood must overleap the bounds
Of lineage, transcend Arabia
And Persia: Love's community is like
The light of God; whatever being we
Possess, from its existence is derived.
'None seeketh when or where God's light was born;
What need of warp and woof, God's robe to spin?'
Who suffereth his foot to wear the chains
Of clime and ancestry is unaware
How He begat not, neither was begot?

Iqbal, *The Mysteries of Selflessness*

The Need for Understanding Islam in the Light of Modern Knowledge

During the last five hundred years religious thought in Islam has been practically stationary. There was a time when European thought received inspiration from the world of Islam. The most remarkable phenomenon of modern history, however, is the enormous rapidity with which the world of Islam is spiritually moving towards the West. There is nothing wrong in this movement, for European culture, on its intellectual side, is only a further development of some of the most important phases of the culture of Islam. Our only fear is that the dazzling exterior of European culture may arrest our movement and we may fail to reach the true inwardness of that culture. During all the centuries of our intellectual stupor Europe has been seriously thinking on the great problems in which the philosophers and scientists of Islam were so keenly interested. Since the Middle Ages, when the schools of Muslim theology were completed, infinite advance has taken place in the domain of human thought and experience. The extension of man's power over nature has given him a new faith and a fresh sense of superiority over the forces that constitute his environment. New points of view have been suggested, old problems have been restated in the light of fresh experience and new problems have arisen. It seems as if the intellect of man is outgrowing its own most fundamental categories—time, space and causality. With the advance of scientific thought even our concept of intelligibility is undergoing a change. The theory of Einstein has brought a new vision of the universe and suggests new ways of looking at the problems common to both religion and philosophy. No wonder then that the younger generation of Islam in Asia and Africa demand a fresh orientation of their faith. With the reawakening of Islam, therefore, it is necessary to examine, in an independent spirit, what Europe has thought and how far the conclusions reached by her can help us in the revision and, if necessary, reconstruction, of theological thought in Islam. Besides this it is not possible to ignore the generally antireligious and especially anti-Islamic propaganda in Central Asia which has already crossed the Indian frontier.

The Role of Religion in the World of Today

Thus, wholly overshadowed by the results of his intellectual activity, the modern man has ceased to live soulfully—that is, from within. In the domain of thought he is living in open conflict with himself; and in the domain of economic and political life he is living in open conflict with others. He finds himself unable to control his ruthless egoism and his infinite gold-hunger which is gradually killing all higher striving in him and bringing him nothing but life-weariness. Absorbed in the 'fact' that is to say, the optically present source of sensation, he is entirely cut off from the unplumbed depths of his own being. In the wake of his systematic materialism has at last come that paralysis of energy which Huxley apprehended and deplored. The condition of things in the East is no better. The technique of medieval mysticism by which religious life, in its higher manifestations, developed itself both in the East and in the West has now practically failed. And in the Muslim East it has, perhaps, done far greater havoc than anywhere else. Far from reintegrating the forces of the average man's inner life, and thus preparing him for participation in the march of history, it has taught him a false renunciation and made him perfectly contented with his ignorance and spiritual thralldom. No wonder then that the modern Muslim in Turkey, Egypt, and Persia is led to seek fresh sources of energy in the creation of new loyalties, such as patriotism and nationalism which Nietzsche described as 'sickness and unreason,' and 'the strongest force against culture'. Disappointed with a purely religious method of spiritual renewal which alone brings us into touch with the everlasting fountain of life and power by expanding our thought and emotion, the modern Muslim fondly hopes to unlock fresh sources of energy by narrowing down his thought and emotion. Modern atheistic socialism, which possesses all the fervour of a new religion, has a broader outlook; but having received its philosophical basis from the Hegelians of the left wing, it rises in revolt against the very source which could have given it strength and purpose. Both nationalism and atheistic socialism, at least in the present state of human adjustments, must draw upon the psychological forces of hate, suspicion, and resentment which tend to impoverish the soul of man and close up his hidden sources of spiritual energy. Neither the technique of medieval mysticism nor nationalism nor atheistic socialism can cure the ills of a despairing humanity. Surely the present moment is one of great crisis in the history of modern culture. The modern world stands in need of biological renewal. And religion, which in its higher manifestations is neither dogma, nor priesthood, nor ritual, can alone ethically prepare the modern man for the burden of the great responsibility which the advancement of modern science necessarily involves, and restore him that attitude of faith which makes him capable of winning a personality here and retaining it hereafter. It is only by rising to a fresh vision of his origin and future, his whence and whither, that man will eventually triumph over a society motivated by an inhuman competition, and a civilization which has lost its spiritual unity by its inner conflict of religious and political values.

Iqbal, *Reconstruction of Religious Thought in Islam*

Islam and Human Dignity

The present struggle in India is sometimes described as India's revolt against the West. I do not think it is a revolt against the West; for the people of India are demanding the very institutions which the West stands for . . . Educated urban India demands democracy. The minorities, feeling themselves as distinct cultural units and fearing that their very existence is at stake, demand safeguards, which the majority community, for obvious reasons, refuses to concede. The majority community pretends to believe in a nationalism theoretically correct, if we start from Western premises, belied by facts, if we look to India. Thus the real parties to the present struggle in India are not England and India, but the majority community and the minorities of India which can ill afford to accept the principle of Western democracy until it is properly modified to suit the actual conditions of life in India.

Nor do Mahatma Gandhi's political methods signify a revolt in the psychological sense. These methods arise out of a contact of two opposing types of world-consciousness, Western and Eastern. The Western man's mental texture is chronological in character. He lives and moves and has his being in time. The Eastern man's world-consciousness is nonhistorical. To the Western man things gradually become; they have a past, present and future. To the Eastern man they are immediately rounded off, timeless, purely present. That is why Islam which sees in the time-movement a symbol of reality appeared as an intruder in the static world-pictures of Asia. The British as a Western people cannot but conceive political reform in India as a systematic process of gradual evolution. Mahatma Gandhi as an Eastern man sees in this attitude nothing more than an ill-conceived unwillingness to part with power and tries all sorts of destructive negations to achieve immediate attainment. Both are elementally incapable of understanding each other. The result is the appearance of a revolt.

These phenomena, however, are merely premonitions of a coming storm, which is likely to sweep over the whole of India and the rest of Asia. This is the inevitable outcome of a wholly political civilization which has looked upon man as a *thing* to be exploited and not as a *personality* to be developed and enlarged by purely cultural forces. The peoples of Asia are bound to rise against the acquisitive economy which the West has developed and imposed on the nations of the East. Asia cannot comprehend modern Western capitalism with its undisciplined individualism. The faith which you represent recognizes the worth of the individual, and disciplines him to give away his all to the service of God and man. Its possibilities are not yet exhausted. It can still create a new world where the social rank of man is not determined by his caste or colour, or the amount of dividend he earns, but by the kind of life he lives; where the poor tax the rich, where human society is founded not on the equality of stomachs but on the equality of spirits, where an untouchable can marry the daughter of a king, where private ownership is a trust and where capital cannot be allowed to accumulate so as to dominate the real producer of wealth. This superb idealism of your faith, however, needs emancipation from the medieval fancies of theologians and legists. Spiritually we are living in a prison-house of thoughts and emotions which during the course of centuries we have woven round ourselves. And be it further said to the shame of us—men of [the] older generation—that we have failed to equip the younger generation for the economic, political and even religious crises that the present age is likely to bring. The whole community needs a complete overhauling of its present mentality in order that it may again become capable of feeling the urge of fresh desires and ideals. The Indian Muslim has long ceased to explore the depths of his own inner life. The result is that he has ceased to live in the full glow and colour of life, and is consequently in danger of an unmanly compromise with forces which, he is made to think, he cannot vanquish in open conflict. He who desires to change an unfavourable environment must undergo a complete transformation of his inner being. God changeth not the condition of a people until they themselves take the initiative to change their condition by constantly illuminating the zone of their daily activity in the light of a definite ideal. Nothing can be achieved without a firm faith in the independence of one's own inner life. This faith alone keeps a people's eye fixed on their goal and saves them from perpetual vacillation . . . The flame of life cannot be borrowed from others; it must be kindled in the temple of one's own soul.

Iqbal, *Speeches and Statements*

MAULANA ABUL KALAM AZAD

Maulana Abul Kalam Muhiyuddin Ahmed (11 November 1888–22 February 1958) was a prominent leader of the Indian independence movement. He was one of the most prominent Muslim leaders to support Hindu-Muslim unity, and opposed the partition of India on communal lines. Following India's independence, he became the first education minister in the Indian government. He adopted 'Azad' (Free) as his pen-name.

Letter 13

Ahmad Nagar Fort
18 October 1942

Dear Friend,

What I wrote yesterday was finished on paper but its theme lingered in the mind. Now that I picked up the pen the mind began to move in the same direction.

This level of thought directs our attention towards another reality. Why could man not rest content with metarational and impersonal concept of God and continue to create a personal concept according to his thoughts and feelings? I am using the expression 'personal' in the same sense that we use the term 'Personal God'. There are different stages of personal concept. The elementary stage is just a person who only confirms the personality. Subsequently this personality acquires certain aspects of specific qualities and activities. Why was this development inevitable? The reason is the same that by nature man needs a higher goal and the thirst for that is not satisfied without a concept indicating personality and its relationships. Whatever the reality when it is seen it comes wearing a personal mask. This mask was at times thick and heavy and sometimes light, at times frightening and at other times pleasing. But it never fell from the face. From here starts all the troubles of our image-worshipping proclivity:

> Bar chehra-e-haqiqat agar mand pardai
> Jurm-e-nigah-e-suratparast-e-maa-st

(If reality wears a mask on its face,
It is the fault of my image-worshipping tendency.)

India is the oldest source of Pantheism. Most probably it reached Greece and Alexandria also from here and Neo-Platonism (which the Arabs mistakenly thought the religion of Plato) built its oriental superstructure on its foundation. This belief purifies the concept of all personal traits and imparts it the quality of absolute perfection. This concept does not admit of image quality, and if at all in the form of determinants and appearances, not as the personality of the Absolute One. Its believer cannot say anything about Him except that He 'is', that's all. He cannot give even a hint. If we allow even the shadow of our hints the Absolute One does not remain absolute and is covered in the dust of identity and limitations. Baba Faghani has said everything in the two lines of this verse:

> Mushkil hikayat-st keh har zarra ain-e-oo-st
> amma nami tuwan keh isharat b'oo kunan

(It's difficult to believe that every particle is exactly He,

But I don't have the ability to even indicate that.)

That is why Indian Upanishads have adopted negativism and have carried the purificatory process of 'not this, not this' very far. But see, the same India to quench its thirst not only began to see *Brhma* (the Absolute One) in the form of *Ishwar* (the One with human quality) but also started keeping stone images in front so that there is something for the mind to concentrate on:

> *Kare kya Kaba meinjo sare butkhana se aagah hai*
> *Yahaan to koi surat bhi hai,van allah hi allah hai*

(One used to the sacrament of temple can find no satisfaction in Kaba;
The temple has at least some images; there is nothing except invisible Allah.)

The Jews viewed God as a tyrannical and oppressive despot whose relation with the Israeli family was like that of a high-minded husband with his favourite wife. The husband would excuse all the faults of his wife but not her betrayal because his sense of honour does not tolerate that someone else should share his love. A verse in Qur'an also says: 'God does not forgive the sin of making somebody share his lofty position though He does at His discretion pardon all other sins.' (Maulana's Urdu translation from the original Arabic). One of the Ten Commandments of Torat was: 'Do not make a statue of anything, nor bow before anyone else because I, your God, am jealous of my honour.' With passage of time this concept developed more breadth and kindness. By the time of Isaiah

II there began to develop the concept that later took the form of Christianity that saw Father in place of husband because the father is all kindness and affection for his children and an embodiment of forgiveness:

> Man bad kunam v tu bad makafat dahi
> Pasfarq myan-e-man v' tu chee-st

(My deed was bad, so was your retribution;
What then is the difference between you and me?)

Islam based its faith entirely on exclusivity. In a verse in Qur'an it is said 'There is none like Him.' Simile has been so sweepingly prohibited that nothing is left for our personal image: 'Do not fix similarities upon Him.' All openings to simile are closed with the assertion: 'Our sight cannot reach Him, eyes cannot catch Him.' and '(God told Moosa) You cannot see me at all; look towards the mountain.' This left no further scope for sensory perception of reality:

> Zabaan b'band v nazar baaz kun keh mana'-e-Kaleem
> ishaarat az adab aamozi taqaza-e-st

(Close lips, turn away eyes, for God's interlocutor has prohibited all sound and sight;
The demand is to learn from signs only.)

Still for communication of concepts he too had to resort to imagery and the exclusive Absolute took on the apparel of personal qualities as a verse in Qur'an says: 'All names of God are equally good; use those names to call Him.' And then it did not stop there. Reward and punishment also made appearance here and there. A verse, for example, reads: 'Both His hands

are open, for reward and punishment.' and 'On their hands
there is God Almighty's own hand', and, 'When you threw
a handful of stones, they had not been cast by you but by
Allah Himself,. And that 'That all merciful God has His seat
in Heaven' and that 'Sure your God is on prowl.' and 'Every
day that rises reflects His glory':

> Harchand ho mushahida-e-haq ki guftgu
> Banti naheen hai baada-o-saghar kahe b'ghair

(Even if the talk is about perception of reality,
Communication is impossible without reference to cup
and wine.)

That shows that the urge for a lofty goal is a natural human
urge that cannot be satisfied until the concept appears in some
concrete form and that is possible only if the abstract and
impersonal face wears the mask of personality:

> Aah azaan hausla-e-tang v azaan husn-e-buland
> Keh dilam ra gila az hasrat-e deedar-e-tu ne-sf-

(Alas, courage is limited and beauty on a lofty height
The mind does not even complain of the desire to see
you.)

Human mind cannot capture a concept without attributes
and the desire is for what can be captured. He wants a view of
the beloved that can capture his heart, whose shy beauty may
compel passionate pursuit, to hold whose magnificent apparel
he may extend his hand of humility and prayer, with whom
he may spend nights exchanging secrets of love, who may be
at the loftiest height but from there must be casting glances,

that: 'Your God is all the time watching you' and 'O Prophet, if my people question you, (tell them) when am I away from you? I respond to every one who calls me.'

> *Darpardai v bar hama kasparda mee dart*
> *Baa har kasi v baa tu kase ra vasaal ne-st*

> (From behind the veil you keep watch on all,
> No one however has access to you.)

Abstract concept is only negative but concrete concept, in negating likeness, produces a positive picture. That is why here also attributes were imagined. That is why ancient Islamic *ulama* and experts on *hadith* took recourse to reference and shied away from interpretation of attributes; that is why they explained abstractionism of Nehemiah as suspension and sensed the same in the exegeses of Muslim rationalists and scholastic philosophers of Islam. The schoolmen had accused the followers *of hadith* of anthropomorphism but the latter replied: our so-called anthropomorphism is better than your abstractionism; in our concept there is some basis left for a concept but your exclusivism and negativism leaves one hanging in the air.

The declensions that the *Upanishads* of India have sketched while converting the abstract One into anthropomorphic God, Muslim *sufis* saw in Unitarian and monotheistic concepts of God. Unitarian concept means absolute, unshared oneness while monotheism only asserts primary position and admits of a second, third, fourth etc. . . is not *Hadith of Qudsi* but whoever be the author it reflects deep thought:

> *Dil kushta-e-yaktai-e-husn ast, vagarna*
> *Dar pesh-e-tu aaina shikastan hunre bood*[21]

> (My heart is smitten with thy unique beauty,
> Otherwise breaking the mirror before you was an
> art.)

I have touched upon this issue in *Tarjamanul Qur'an*, in the context of the interpretation of *Sura Fatiha* in volume I and, in volume II. . . The issue is such that if dilated upon it is capable of tremendous expansion:

> *Talqeen-e-dars-e-ahl-nazaryak isharat-st*
> *kardam isharte v mukarram nami kunam*

> (A hint is enough to teach the wise;
> I give the hint and repeat not.)

In this discussion another issue arises that extends its reach pretty far. If there exists nothing except matter, then what is the power that arises at the human stage of being and that we call thought and comprehension? From which stove did this ember fly? What is it that imparts to us the ability to contemplate the essence of matter itself and pass all kinds of verdicts on it? It is true that this quality also, as in other beings, developed gradually and remained dormant in vegetable form. Its first stirrings appeared in animals and fully awakened at the stage of human being. But this knowledge of the process does not help us untangle this enigma. The seed sprouted all of a sudden or arrived at this stage after a long process of development; in any case it is the essence of the human condition and is distinct and superior to all other beings that exist in terms of essence and manifestation. This is the point where humankind separated from all other links in the chain of development and the desire for power to grow into a higher form began to stir in him. Sitting as the lord of this world when he looks up he thinks all the planetary beings he sees are meant for him. He measures and studies them and forms opinion about their character and conduct. At every step he has to acknowledge his limitations in comparison with the unlimited reach of Nature's workshop. This sense of limitation however does not depress his aspirations to try and desire. Rather they flourish with greater vigour and seek to carry him to loftier heights. What is this unlimited atmosphere that flies man around? Is it enough to say that it is a blind and deaf force that developed from its natural state and attributes into the blazing flame of thought and perception? People not used to seeing beyond the material frame too would not dare an unhesitating response to this question.

I do not want to refer here to the revolution that began to take shape in the closing years of the nineteenth century and that, at the outset of the twentieth century, shook all the basic notions of classical physics. I am trying to look at the problem from a commoner's angle, keeping away from that.

Moreover, what is that which we term as evolution? And, why is it so? Is it not pointing its finger in a particular direction? After centuries of search we discovered that all we see in its present form before us did not appear all of a sudden. In other words, they were not given their present form and character by a direct creative process; rather, a universal principle of gradual change has been at work and, everything keeps changing in accordance with this principle. Every thing changes at a pace so slow that we cannot measure it on the scale even of planetary figures. From the lowest particles to the heavenly bodies, every thing has evolved into its present shape and character in accordance with this principle of change and transformation. This is the low-to-high pace of Nature that we call evolution.

Or, a definite, well-planned, harmonious and organized urge is taking the universe in a particular direction. Every lower link gradually evolves into its higher link, and, every higher form influences the progress of the lower and casts it in a particular mould. This evolutionary process is not self-explanatory; it needs explaining but no materialist explanation is available. The question is why should there be this evolutionary urge that pushes every creative manifestation from lower to higher stages? Why did the nature of being develop the urge to rise higher so that there is a well-organized ascent of the complex of beings in which every step is higher than the previous one and lower than the next? Is all this without any meaning and significance? Has this staircase come to be without any upper storey and is there no lofty roof towards which it seeks to take us?

Yaaran, khabar diked keh een jalwagah-e-kee-st?

(Friends, tell me whose manifestation all this is?)

Among our contemporary biologists, Prof. Lloyd Morgan has attempted a deep study of the issue from the biological viewpoint but he too has arrived at the conclusion that there can be no materialist explanation for it. He writes that the resultants that we see in operation can be explained by way of calling them the result of visible conditions. But the emergence of the evolutionary urge like the appearance of life, the majesty of perception and comprehension, and the moulding of mental identity and meaningful individuality cannot be explained without recognizing the operation of a godly power. This situation forces us ultimately not to shrink from belief in the working of a creative principle, an essential creativity which is the timeless reality in this network of time and space.

While studying the facts of existence it strikes us that the system of Nature is such that its reality cannot be perceived unless seen from a higher plane. In other words, to see each order of Nature we have to position ourselves at a higher point of view. The subtleties of physics are revealed by biology and those of biology by psychology. And, to understand the subtleties of psychology we have to take recourse to reason and analysis. Now, from what point should we view the problems arising from reason and analysis? Is there or is there not a point higher than that which could take us to the final reality?

We have to acknowledge that there does exist a higher viewpoint but that is at such a lofty height that it is beyond reason and analysis to sketch out. That is supra-sensible although it is not elusive of senses. It is a fire that cannot be seen but can provide warmth to hands: 'One who has not tasted cannot know.'

> *Tu nazar baaz na-i, varna taghafal nigah-st*
> *Tu zabanfahm na-i, varna khamoshi sukhn-st*

(You do not understand sight, otherwise indifference is attention;
You understand not language, otherwise silence is eloquence.)

The universe is not static but mobile and keeps developing and progressing in a definite direction. Its inherent character is in every sense constructive and perfectionist. If we do not get materialistic explanation for this universal process of development and progress, we are not wrong in looking for a solution of the problem in spiritualism.

At this juncture we should also bear in mind that the beliefs that were generated by eighteenth and nineteenth centuries began to shake at the outset of this century; solid matter has yielded place to ethereal force. Discussion on the quantum of characteristics, actions and reach of electrons has shifted the issue from the sphere of science to that of philosophy. The confidence that science had in its knowledge and discipline has been completely shaken and knowledge has again entered the domain of subjective sphere of mental formulations from where it had departed and launched on a new journey during the period of renaissance. I will however not touch this discussion now because that is by itself a continuing controversy.

It is true that this road cannot be covered merely by reasoned knowledge. Here light is provided by revelation and perception. If we do not want to get into that world, you can see manifestations of reality all around you; our existence itself is a manifest guide.

> khalqe nishan-e-dost talab mee kunand-o-baaz
> Az dost ghafil and b'chundeen nishan keh hast

> (People look for a sign of the friend, but then
> Being indifferent to the friend how can they see the sign?)

Abul Kalam

JAWAHARLAL NEHRU

*Jawaharlal Nehru (14 November 1889–27 May 1964) was a
freedom fighter and the first prime minister of independent India.
He is also referred to as Panditji or scholar. Nehru's appreciation
of the virtues of parliamentary democracy, secularism and
liberalism, coupled with his concerns for the poor and
underprivileged, are recognized to have guided him in formulating
policies that influence India to this day.*

A Tryst with Destiny

Long years ago we made a tryst with destiny, and now the
time comes when we shall redeem our pledge, not wholly or
in full measure, but very substantially. At the stroke of the
midnight hour, when the world sleeps, India will awake to
life and freedom. A moment comes, which comes but rarely
in history, when we step out from the old to the new, when
an age ends, and when the soul of a nation, long suppressed,
finds utterance. It is fitting that at this solemn moment we
take the pledge of dedication to the service of India and her
people and to the still larger cause of humanity.

At the dawn of history India started on her unending
quest, and trackless centuries are filled with her striving and
the grandeur of her successes and her failures. Through good
and ill fortune alike she has never lost sight of that quest or
forgotten the ideals which gave her strength. We end today
a period of ill fortune and India discovers herself again. The

achievement we celebrate today is but a step, an opening of opportunity to the greater triumphs and achievements that await us. Are we brave enough and wise enough to grasp this opportunity and accept the challenge of the future?

Freedom and power bring responsibility. That responsibility rests upon this Assembly, a sovereign body representing the sovereign people of India. Before the birth of freedom we have endured all the pains of labour and our hearts are heavy with the memory of this sorrow. Some of those pains continue even now. Nevertheless, the past is over and it is the future that beckons to us now.

That future is not one of ease or resting but of incessant striving so that we might fulfil the pledges we have so often taken and the one we shall take today. The service of India means the service of the millions who suffer. It means the ending of poverty and ignorance and disease and inequality of opportunity. The ambition of the greatest man of our generation has been to wipe every tear from every eye. That may be beyond us but as long as there are tears and suffering, so long our work will not be over.

And so we have to labour and to work and work hard to give reality to our dreams. Those dreams are for India, but they are also for the world for all the nations and peoples are too closely knit together today for any one of them to imagine that it can live apart. Peace has been said to be indivisible, so is freedom, so is prosperity now, and so also is disaster in this one world that can no longer be split into isolated fragments.

To the people of India, whose representatives we are, we make appeal to join us with faith and confidence in this great adventure. This is no time for petty and destructive criticism, no time for ill will or blaming others. We have to build the noble mansion of free India where all her children may dwell.

I beg to move, Sir, that it be resolved that:

1 After the last stroke of midnight, all members of the Constituent Assembly present on this occasion do take the following pledge:

At this solemn moment when the people of India, through suffering and sacrifice, have secured freedom, I, a member of the Constituent Assembly of India, do dedicate myself in all humility to the service of India and her people to the end that this ancient land attain her rightful place in the world and make her full and willing contribution to the promotion of world peace and the welfare of mankind.

2 Members who are not present on this occasion do take the pledge (with such verbal changes as the President may prescribe) at the time they next attend a session of the Assembly.

The Light Has Gone Out

The light has gone out from our lives and there is darkness everywhere. And I do not know what to tell you and how to say it. Our beloved leader, Bapu, as we called him, the Father of the Nation, is no more. Perhaps I am wrong to say that. Nevertheless, we will not see him again as we have seen him for these many years. We will not run to him for advice and seek solace from him; and that is a terrible blow, not to me only, but to millions and millions in this country. And it is a little difficult to soften the blow by any advice that I or anyone else can give you.

The light has gone out, I said, and yet I was wrong. For the light that shone in this country was no ordinary light. The light that has illumined this country for these many, many years will illumine this country for many more years, and a thousand years later that light will still be seen in this country, and the world will see it, and it will give solace to innumerable hearts. For that light represented something more than the immediate present; it represented the living, eternal truths reminding us of the right path, drawing us from errors, taking this ancient country to freedom.

All this has happened when there was so much more for him to do. We could never, of course, do away with him, we could never think that he was unnecessary, or that he had done his task. But how, particularly, when we are faced with so many difficulties, his not being with us is a blow most terrible to bear.

A mad man has put an end to his life, for I can only call him mad who did it. And yet there has been enough of poison spread in this country during the past years and months, and this poison has had effect on people's minds. We must face this poison, we must root out this poison, and we must face all the perils that encompass us, and face them, not madly or badly, but rather in the way that our beloved teacher taught us to face them. The first thing to remember now is that none of us dare misbehave because we are angry. We have to behave like strong, determined people, determined to face all the perils that surround us, determined to carry out the mandate that our great teacher and our great leader has given us, remembering always that if, as I believe, his spirit looks upon us and sees us, nothing would displease his soul so much as to see that we have indulged in unseemly behaviour or in violence. So we must not do that. But that does not mean that we should be weak, but rather that we should, in strength and in unity, face all the troubles that are in front of us. We must hold together, and all our petty troubles and difficulties and conflicts must be ended in the face of this great disaster. A great disaster is a symbol to us to remember all the big things of life and forget the small things of which we have thought too much. Now the time has come again. As in his life, so in his death he has reminded us of the big things of life, the living truth, and if we remember that, then it will be well with us and well with India.

May I now tell you the programme for tomorrow? It was proposed by some friends that Mahatmaji's body should be embalmed for a few days to enable millions of people to pay their last homage to him. But it was his wish, repeatedly expressed, that no such thing should happen, that this should not be done, that he was entirely opposed to any embalming of his body, and so we decided that we must follow his wishes in this matter, however much others might have wished otherwise.

And so the cremation will take place tomorrow in Delhi city by the side of the Jumna river. Tomorrow morning, or rather forenoon, about 11.30, the bier will be taken out from Birla House and it will follow the prescribed route and go to the Jumna river. The cremation will take place there at about 4.00 p.m. The exact place and route will be announced by radio and the press.

People in Delhi who wish to pay their last homage should gather along this route. I would not advise too many of them to come to Birla House, but rather to gather on both sides of this long route, from Birla House to the Jumna river. And I trust that they will remain there in silence without any demonstrations. That is the best way and the most fitting way to pay homage to this great soul. Also, tomorrow should be a day of fasting and prayer for all of us.

Those who live elsewhere, out of Delhi and in other parts of India, will no doubt also take such part as they can in this last homage. For them also let this be a day of fasting and prayer. And at the appointed time for cremation, that is 4.00 p.m. tomorrow afternoon, people should go to the river or to the sea and offer prayers there. And while we pray, the greatest prayer that we can offer is to take a pledge to dedicate ourselves to the truth and to the cause for which this great countryman of ours lived and for which he has died. That is the best prayer that we can offer him and his memory. That is the best prayer that we can offer to India and ourselves. *Jai Hind*.

Will and Testament

I have received so much love and affection from the Indian people that nothing that I can do can repay even a small fraction of it, and indeed there can be no repayment of so precious a thing as affection. Many have been admired, some have been revered, but the affection of all classes of the Indian people has come to me in such abundant measure that I have been overwhelmed by it. I can only express the hope that in the remaining years I may live, I shall not be unworthy of my people and their affection.

To my innumerable comrades and colleagues, I owe an even deeper debt of gratitude. We have been joint partners in great undertakings and have shared the triumphs and sorrows which inevitably accompany them.

I wish to declare with all earnestness that I do not want any religious ceremonies performed for me after my death. I do not believe in any such ceremonies and to submit to them, even as a matter of form, would be hypocrisy and an attempt to delude ourselves and others.

When I die, I should like my body to be cremated. If I die in a foreign country, my body should be cremated there and my ashes sent to Allahabad. A small handful of these ashes should be thrown into the Ganga and the major portion of them disposed of in the manner indicated below. No part of these ashes should be retained or preserved.

My desire to have a handful of my ashes thrown into the Ganga at Allahabad has no religious significance, so far as I am concerned. I have no religious sentiment in the matter. I have been attached to the Ganga and the Jumna rivers in Allahabad ever since my childhood and, as I have grown older, this attachment has also grown. I have watched their varying moods as the seasons changed, and have often thought of the history and myth and tradition, and song and story, that have become attached to them through the long ages and become a part of their flowing waters. The Ganga, especially, is the river of India, beloved of her people, round which are intertwined her racial memories, her hopes and fears, her songs of triumph, her victories and her defeats. She has been a symbol of India's age-long culture and civilization, ever-changing, ever-flowing, and yet ever the same Ganga. She reminds me of the snow-covered peaks and the deep valleys of the Himalayas, which I have loved so much, and of the rich and vast plains below, where my life and work have been cast. Smiling and dancing in the morning sunlight, and dark and gloomy and full of mystery as the evening shadows fall, a narrow, slow and graceful stream in winter, and a vast roaring thing during the monsoon, broad-bosomed almost as the sea, and with something of the sea's power to destroy, the Ganga has been to me a symbol and a memory of the past of India, running into the present, and flowing on to the great ocean of the future. And though I have discarded much of past tradition and custom, and am anxious that India should rid herself of all shackles that bind and constrain her and divide her people, and suppress vast numbers of them, and prevent the free development of the body and the spirit; though I seek all this, yet I do not wish to cut myself off from that past completely. I am proud of that great inheritance that has been, and is, ours, and I am conscious that I too, like all of us, am a link in that unbroken chain which goes back to the dawn of history in the immemorial past of India. That chain I would not break, for I treasure it and seek inspiration from it. And as witness of this desire of mine and as my last homage to India's cultural inheritance, I am making this request that a handful of my ashes be thrown into the Ganga at Allahabad to be carried to the great ocean that washes India's shore. The major portion of my ashes should, however, be disposed of otherwise. I want these to be carried high up into the air in an aeroplane and scattered from that height over the fields where the peasants of India toil, so that they might mingle with the dust and soil of India and become an indistinguishable part of India.

J. KRISHNAMURTI

Jiddu Krisnamurti (12 May 1895–17 February 1986) was a renowned writer and speaker on philosophical and spiritual subjects. He stressed the need for a revolution in the psyche of every human being to bring about any change, religious, political or social.

What Are We Seeking?

What is it that most of us are seeking? What is it that each one of us wants? Surely it is important to find out. Probably most of us are seeking some kind of happiness, some kind of peace; in a world that is ridden with turmoil, wars, contention, strife, we want a refuge where there can be some peace. I think that is what most of us want. So we pursue, go from one leader to another, from one religious organization to another, from one teacher to another.

Now, is it that we are seeking happiness or is it that we are seeking gratification of some kind from which we hope to derive happiness? There is a difference between happiness and gratification. Can you *seek* happiness? Perhaps you can find gratification but surely you cannot *find* happiness. Happiness is derivative; it is a by-product of something else. So, before we give our minds and hearts to something which demands a great deal of earnestness, attention, thought, care, we must find out, must we not, what it is that we are seeking; whether it is happiness or gratification. I am afraid most of us are seeking gratification. We want to be gratified, we want to find a sense of fullness at the end of our search.

After all, if one is seeking peace one can find it very easily. One can devote oneself blindly to some kind of cause, to an idea, and take shelter there. Surely that does not solve the problem. Mere isolation in an enclosing idea is not a release from conflict. So we must find, must we not, what it is, inwardly, as well as outwardly, that each one of us wants. If we are clear on that matter, then we don't have to go anywhere, to any teacher, to any church, to any organization. But our difficulty is to be clear in ourselves regarding our intention. Can we be clear? And does that clarity come through searching, through trying to find out what others say, from the highest teacher to the ordinary preacher in a church round the corner? Have you got to go to somebody to find out? Yet that is what we are doing, is it not? We read innumerable books, we attend many meetings and discuss, we join various organizations—trying thereby to find a remedy to the conflict, to the miseries in our lives. Or, if we don't do all that, we think we have found; that is, we say that a particular organization, a particular teacher, a particular book satisfies us; we have found everything we want in that; and we remain in that, crystallized and enclosed.

Do we not seek, through all this confusion, something permanent, something lasting, something which we call real?—God, truth, what you like—the name doesn't matter, the word is not the thing, surely. So don't let us be caught in words. Leave that to the professional lecturers. There is a search for something permanent, is there not, in most of us—something we can cling to, something which will give us assurance, a hope, a lasting enthusiasm, a lasting certainty, because in ourselves we are so uncertain. We do not know ourselves. We know a lot about facts, what the books have said; but we do not know for ourselves, we do not have a direct experience.

And what is it that we call permanent? What is it that we are seeking, which will, or which we hope will give us permanency? Are we not seeking lasting happiness, lasting gratification, lasting certainty? We want something that will endure everlastingly, which will gratify us. If we strip ourselves of all the words and phrases, and actually look at it, this is what we want. We want permanent pleasure, permanent gratification—which we call truth, God or what you will.

Very well, we want pleasure. Perhaps that may be putting it very crudely, but that is actually what we want—knowledge that will give us pleasure, experience that will give us pleasure, a gratification that will not wither away by tomorrow. And we have experimented with various gratifications, and they have all faded away; and we hope now to find permanent gratification in reality, in God. Surely, that is what we are all seeking—the clever ones and the stupid ones, the theorist and the factual person who is striving after something. And is there permanent gratification? Is there something which will endure?

Now, if you seek permanent gratification, surely you must understand, must you not, the thing you are seeking. When you say, 'I am seeking permanent happiness'—God, or truth, or what you like—must you not also understand the thing that is searching, the searcher, the seeker? Because there may be no such thing as permanent security, permanent happiness. Truth may be something entirely different; and I think it is utterly different from what you can see, conceive, formulate. Therefore, before we seek something permanent, is it not obviously necessary to understand the seeker? Is the seeker different from the thing he seeks? When you say, 'I am seeking happiness', is the seeker different from the object of his search?

Is the thinker different from the thought? Are they not a joint phenomenon, rather than separate processes? Therefore it is essential, is it not, to understand the seeker, before you try to find out what it is he is seeking.

So we have to come to the point when we ask ourselves, really earnestly and profoundly, if peace, happiness, reality, God, or what you will, can be given to us by someone else. Can this incessant search, this longing, give us that extraordinary sense of reality, that creative being, which comes when we really understand ourselves? Does self-knowledge come through search, through following someone else, through belonging to any particular organization, through reading books, and so on? After all, that is the main issue, is it not, that so long as I do not understand myself, I have no basis for thought, and all my search will be in vain. I can escape into illusions; I can run away from contention, strife, struggle; I can worship another; I can look for my salvation through somebody else. But so long as I am ignorant of myself, so long as I am unaware of the total process of myself, I have no basis for thought, for affection, for action.

But that is the last thing we want: to know ourselves. Yet that is the only foundation on which we can build. Before we can build, before we can transform, before we can condemn or destroy, we must know that which we are. If we are petty, jealous, vain, greedy—*that* is what we create about us, *that* is the society in which we live.

It seems to me that before we set out on a journey to find reality, to find God, before we can act, before we can have any relationship with another, which is society, it is essential that we begin to understand ourselves first. I consider the earnest person to be one who is completely concerned with this, *first*, and not with how to arrive at a particular goal, because, if you and I do not understand ourselves, how can we, in action, bring about a transformation in society, in relationship, in anything that we do? And it does not mean, obviously, that self-knowledge is opposed to, or isolated from, relationship. It does not mean, obviously, emphasis on the individual, the me, as opposed to the mass, as opposed to another.

Now without knowing yourself, without knowing your own way of thinking and why you think certain things, without knowing the background of your conditioning and why you have certain beliefs about art and religion, about your country and your neighbour and about yourself, how can you think truly about anything? Without knowing your background, without knowing the substance of your thought and whence it comes—surely your search is utterly futile, your action has no meaning?

Before we can find out what the end-purpose of life is, what it all means—wars, national antagonisms, conflicts, the whole mess—we must begin with ourselves, must we not? It sounds so simple, but it is *extremely* difficult. To follow oneself, to see how one's thought operates, one has to be extraordinarily alert, so that as one begins to be more and more alert to the intricacies of one's own thinking and responses and feelings, one begins to have a greater awareness, not only of oneself but of another with whom one is in relationship. To know oneself is to study oneself in action, which is relationship. The difficulty is that we are so impatient; we want to get on, we want to reach an end, and so we have neither the time nor the occasion to give ourselves the opportunity to study, to observe. Alternatively, we have committed ourselves to various activities—to earning a livelihood, to rearing children—or have taken on certain responsibilities of various organizations; we have so committed ourselves in different ways that we have hardly any time for self-reflection, to observe, to study. So really the responsibility of the reaction depends on oneself, not on another. The pursuit, all the world over, of *gurus* and their systems, reading the latest books on this and that, and so on, seems to me so utterly empty, so utterly futile, for you may wander all over the earth but you have to come back to yourself. And, as most of us are totally unaware of ourselves, it is extremely difficult to begin to see clearly the process of our thinking and feeling and acting.

The more you know yourself, the more clarity there is. Self-knowledge has no end—you don't come to an achievement, you don't come to a conclusion. It is an endless river. As one studies it, as one goes into it more and more, one finds peace. Only when the mind is tranquil—through self-knowledge and not through imposed self-discipline—only then, in that tranquility, in that silence, can reality come into being. It is only then that there can be bliss, that there can be creative action. And it seems to me that without this understanding, without this experience, merely to read books, to attend talks, to do propaganda, is so infantile—just an activity without much meaning; whereas if one is able to understand oneself, and thereby bring about that creative happiness, that experiencing of something that is not of the mind, then perhaps there can be a transformation in the immediate relationship about us and so in the world in which we live.

For the young

Have you ever wondered why it is that as people grow older they seem to lose all joy in life? At present most of you who are young are fairly happy; you have your little problems, there are examinations to worry about, but in spite of these troubles there is in your life a certain joy, is there not? There is a spontaneous, easy acceptance of life, a looking at things lightly and happily. And why it is that as we grow older we seem to lose that joyous intimation of something beyond, something of greater significance? Why do so many of us, as we grow into so-called maturity, become dull, insensitive to joy, to beauty, to the open skies and the marvellous earth?

You know, when one asks oneself this question, many explanations spring up in the mind. We are so concerned with ourselves—that is one explanation. We struggle to become somebody, to achieve and maintain a certain position; we have children and other responsibilities, and we have to earn money. All these external things soon weigh us down, and thereby we lose the joy of living. Look at the older faces around you, see how sad most of them are, how careworn and rather ill, how withdrawn, aloof and sometimes neurotic, without a smile. Don't you ask yourself why? And even when we do ask why, most of us seem to be satisfied with mere explanations.

Yesterday evening I saw a boat going up the river at full sail driven by the west wind. It was a large boat, heavily laden with firewood for the town. The sun was setting, and this boat against the sky was astonishingly beautiful The boatman was just guiding it, there was no effort, for the wind was doing all the work. Similarly, if each one of us could understand the problem of struggle and conflict, then I think we would be able to live effortlessly, happily, with a smile on our face.

I think it is effort that destroys us, this struggling in which we spend almost every moment of our lives. If you watch the older people around you, you will see that for most of them life is a series of battles with themselves, with their wives or husbands, with their neighbours, with society; and this ceaseless strife dissipates energy. The man who is joyous, really happy, is not caught up in effort. To be without effort does not mean that you stagnate, that you are dull, stupid; on the contrary, it is only the wise, the extraordinarily intelligent who are really free of effort, struggle.

But, you see, when we hear of effortlessness we want to be like that, we want to achieve a state in which we will have no strife, no conflict; so we make that our goal, our ideal, and strive after it; and the moment we do this, we have lost the joy of living. We are again caught up in effort, struggle. The object of struggle varies, but all struggle is essentially the same. One may struggle to bring about social reforms, or to find God, or to create a better relationship between oneself and one's wife or husband, or with one's neighbour; one may sit on the bank of the Ganges, worship at the feet of some *guru*, and so on. All this is effort, struggle. So what is important is not the object of struggle, but to understand struggle itself.

Now, is it possible for the mind to be not just casually aware that for the moment it is not struggling, but completely free of struggle all the time so that it discovers a state of joy in which there is no sense of the superior and the inferior?

Our difficulty is that the mind feels inferior, and that is why it struggles to be or become something, or to bridge over its various contradictory desires. But don't let us give explanations of why the mind is full of struggle. Every thinking man knows why there is struggle both within and without. Our envy, greed, ambition, our competitiveness leading to ruthless efficiency—these are obviously the factors which cause us to struggle, whether in this world or in the world to come. So we don't have to study psychological books to know why we struggle; and what is important, surely, is to find out if the mind can be totally free of struggle.

After all, when we struggle the conflict is between what we are and what we *should* be or *want* to be. Now, without giving explanations, can one understand this whole process of struggle so that it comes to an end? Like that boat which was moving with the wind, can the mind be without struggle? Surely, this is the question, and not how to achieve a state in which there is no struggle. The very effort to achieve such a state is itself a process of struggle, therefore that state is never achieved. But if you observe from moment to moment how the mind gets caught in everlasting struggle—if you just observe the fact without trying to alter it, without trying to force upon the mind a certain state which you call peace—then you will find that the mind spontaneously ceases to struggle; and in that state it can learn enormously. Learning is then not merely the process of gathering information, but a discovery of the extraordinary riches that lie beyond the scope of the mind; and for the mind that makes this discovery there is joy.

Watch yourself and you will see how you struggle from morning till night, and how your energy is wasted in this struggle. If you merely explain why you struggle, you get lost in explanations and the struggle continues; whereas, if you observe your mind very quietly without giving explanations, if you just let the mind be aware of its own struggle, you will soon find that there comes a state in which there is no struggle at all, but an astonishing watchfulness. In that state of watchfulness there is no sense of the superior and the inferior, there is no big man or little man, there is no *guru*. All those absurdities are gone because the mind is fully wake; and the mind that is fully awake is joyous.

OSHO

Osho (11 December 1931–19 January 1990), also known as Acharya Rajneesh, felt that the modern man is so burdened by archaic traditions of the past and the anxieties of modern-day living that he must go through a deep cleansing process before he could hope to discover the thought-less, relaxed state of meditation.

Life is a Mirror

Once it happened, I was in the mountains with a few friends. We went to see a point known as the Echo Point; it was a beautiful spot, very silent, surrounded by hills. One of the friends started barking like a dog. All the hills echoed it—the whole place appeared as if full of thousands of dogs. Then, somebody else started chanting a Buddhist mantra: *'Sabbe sanghar anichcha. Sabbe dhamma anatta. Gate, gate, para gate, para sangate. Bodhi swaha.'* The hills became Buddhist; they re-echoed it. The mantra means: *'All is impermanent, nothing is permanent; all is flux, nothing is substantial. Everything is without a self. Gone, gone, finally gone, everything gone—the word, the knowledge, the enlightenment too.'*

I told friends who were with me that life is also like this Echo Point: you bark at it, it barks at you; you chant a beautiful mantra, life becomes a reflection of that beautiful chanting. A life is a mirror. Millions of mirrors around you—every face is a mirror; every rock is a mirror; every cloud is a mirror. All relationships are mirrors. In whatsoever way you are related with life, it reflects you. Don't be angry at life if it starts barking at you. You must have started the chain. You must have done something in the beginning to cause it. Don't try to change life; just change yourself, and life changes.

These are two standpoints: one I call the communistic which says, 'Change life, only then can you be happy'; the other I call religious which says, 'Change yourself and life suddenly becomes beautiful.' There is no need to change society, the world. If you move in that direction, you are moving in a false direction which will not lead you anywhere. In the first place, you cannot change it—it is so vast. It is simply impossible. It is so complex and you are here only for a while; and life is very ancient and life is going to be forever and ever. You are just a guest; an overnight stay and you are gone: *gate, gate*—gone, gone forever. How can you imagine to change it?

Sheer stupidity, which says life can be changed, but there is much appeal in it. The communistic standpoint has a deep appeal in it. Not because it is true—the appeal comes from some other source: because it does not make you responsible, that is the appeal. Everything else is responsible except you; you are a victim. 'The whole of life is responsible. Change life'—this is appealing for the ordinary mind because no mind wants to feel responsible.

Whenever you are in misery, you like to throw the responsibility on somebody. Anybody will do, any excuse will do, but then you are unburdened. Now you know you are miserable because of this man or that woman, or this type of society, this government, this social structure, this economy—something—or, finally, God is responsible or fate. These are all communistic standpoints. The moment you throw the responsibility on others, you have become a communist; you are no longer religious.

Even if you throw the responsibility on God, you have become a communist. Try to understand me, because communists don't believe in God, but the whole standpoint of throwing responsibility on somebody else is communistic—then God has to be changed.

That's what people go on doing in temples: they go and pray to change God. Those people are all communists. They may be hiding in religious garbs; they are communists. What are you praying? You are saying to God, 'Do this; don't do that'; 'My wife is ill, make her healthy.' You are telling the whole, 'You are responsible.' You are complaining; deep down your prayer is a complaint. You may be talking very politely, but your politeness is false. You may even be buttering Him up, but deep down you are saying, 'You are responsible—do something!'

This attitude I call the communist attitude; by it I mean the attitude that 'I am not responsible; I am a victim. The whole of life is responsible.' The religious attitude says, 'Life simply reflects.'

Life is not a doer; it is a mirror. It is not doing anything to you, because the same life behaves with Buddha in a different way. The life is the same; it behaves with you in a different way. The mirror is the same, but when you come before the mirror, it reflects your face. And if your face is not that of a Buddha, what can the mirror do? When Buddha comes before the mirror, it reflects Buddhahood.

When I say this to you I say so because that's how I have experienced. Once your face changes, the mirror changes; because a mirror has no fixed standpoint. The mirror is just echoing, reflecting. It does not say anything. It simply shows—it shows you. If life is miserable, you must have started the chain. If everybody is against you, you must have started the chain. If everybody feels enmity, you must have started the chain.

Change the cause. And you are the cause. Religion makes you responsible—and that's how religion makes you free because then it is your freedom to choose. To be miserable or to be happy—it is up to you. Nobody else has anything to do with it. The world will remain the same; you can start dancing, and the whole world dances with you.

They say when you cry, you cry alone, when you laugh, the whole world laughs with you. No, that is also not true. When you cry, the whole world reflects that; when you laugh, then too the whole world reflects that. When you cry, the whole world feels like crying. When you are sad, look at the moon—the moon looks sad; look at the stars—they look like very great pessimists; look at the river—it doesn't seem to flow, gloomy, dark. When you are happy, look at the same moon—it is smiling; and the same stars—dancing; and the same river—flowing with a song, all the gloom has disappeared.

There are no hells and no heavens. When you have a heaven within you, this world . . . And this is the only world there is! Remember, there is no other. When you are filled with heaven within, the world reflects it. When you are filled with hell, the world can't help, it reflects it.

If you yourself feel responsible, you have started moving in a religious direction. Religion believes in individual revolution. There is no other—all others are false, pseudo revolutions. They look like they are changing; they change nothing. They create much fuss about changing—nothing changes. It is not possible to change anything unless you have changed.

These are the sutras about this responsibility: individual responsibility. In the beginning, you will feel a little burdened: that 'I am responsible', and you cannot throw the burden on anybody else. But know well, if you are responsible, there is hope; you can do something. If others are responsible, there is no hope, because what can you do? You may be meditating, but others are creating trouble; you will suffer. You may become a Buddha, but the whole world remains a hell. You will suffer. In the beginning every freedom is felt as a burden—that's why people are afraid of freedom.

Erich Fromm has written a beautiful book, *The Fear of Freedom.* I love the title. Why are people so afraid of freedom? One should think otherwise; they should not be afraid of freedom. On the contrary, we think everybody wants freedom, but this is my observation also: deep down nobody wants freedom—because freedom is a great responsibility. Then only you are responsible. Then you cannot throw responsibility on somebody else's shoulders. Then you don't have any consolation—if you suffer, you suffer for your own causes, for your own self; you have caused it.

But through that burden opens a new door: you can throw it. If I have been causing my miseries, I can stop causing them. I have been pedalling a cycle and I am feeling miserable on the cycle and I am tired, and I go on saying, 'Stop it,' and I go on pedalling. It is for me to stop pedalling, and the cycle stops. Nobody else is pedalling it.

This is the deepest meaning of the theory of karma: that you are responsible. Once you understand it deeply, that 'I am responsible', half the work is done already. In fact, the moment you realize, 'I have been responsible for all that I have been suffering or enjoying', you have become free, free from society, free from the world. Now you can choose your own world to live in. This is the only world—remember! But you can choose now. You can dance, and the whole dances with you.

The Essence of Yoga

SOURCES

A.C. Bose, *Hymns from the Vedas*, Asia Publishing House, 1966.

Theodore de Bary, Stephen N. Hay, Royal Weiler, Andrew Yarrow, eds. *Sources of Indian Tradition*, Volumes I and II, Penguin Books India, 2000.

S. Dhammika, *Ashoka's Edicts*.

Mohandas Karamchand Gandhi, *An Autobiography or The Story of My Experiments with Truth*.

D.R. Goyal, trans. *Sallies of Mind*, Shipra Publications, 2003.

Dr Hadi Hasan, S.A.H. Abidi, A. Schimmel, trans. *Amir Khusrau*.

Juan Mascaró, trans. *The Bhagavad Gita*.

Raimundo Panikkar, trans. *Rig Veda*.

Rabindranath Tagore, trans. *Kabir*.

Rabindranath Tagore, *Sadhana: The Realisation of Life*.

A.K. Ramanujan, trans. *Speaking of Siva*, Penguin Books India, 2007.

213

COPYRIGHT ACKNOWLEDGEMENTS

Grateful acknowledgement is made to the following for permission to reprint copyright material:

Azra Raza and Sara Suleri Goodyear, for the extracts from *Ghalib: Epistemologies of Elegance*, Penguin Books India, 2009.

Indian Council for Cultural Relations (ICCR), for the extracts from *A Treasury of Sanskrit Poetry*, translated by R.S. Pandit, edited by A.N.D. Haksar, ICCR, 2002.

Indira Peterson, for the extracts from *The Rapids of a Great River: The Penguin Book of Tamil Poetry*, edited by Lakshmi Hölmstrom, K. Srilata and Subashree Krishnaswamy, Penguin Books India, 2009.

Khushwant Singh, for the extracts from *Hymns of the Gurus*, Penguin Books India, 2003.

Krishnamurti Foundation Trust, for the extracts from *The Krishnamurti Reader*, edited by Mary Lutyens, Penguin Books India, 2002.

Nilgiri Press for the extracts from *The Upanishads*, translated by Eknath Easwaran, 1991.

Osho International Foundation, for the extracts from *The Essence of Yoga*, Penguin Books India, 2003.

While every effort has been made to trace copyright holders and obtain permission, this has not been possible in all cases; any omissions brought to our attention will be remedied in future editions.